Fruitful Aging

Finding the Gold In
The Golden Years

Tom Pinkson, Ph.D.

ISBN -13:9780-615-78541-7

Email: tompinkson@gmail.com

Websites:
drtompinkson.com,
www.nierica.com

cover photo: Vita Rose

"As someone actively engaged in work for helping create a new, empowering vision for aging in today's world, I have read works by many authors who are also committed to this same goal. This emerging multi-dimensional paradigm has many facets, all important, and fortunately has many writers lending their unique voices and perspectives to this revisioning of what aging can be if approached with consciousness and intentionality. I have learned from many of the books I have read on this subject, with some touching my head and some my heart. Of all these works, Tom Pinkson's Fruitful Aging has been the most impactful for me.

Tom skillfully weaves together concepts, practices, stories of his own growth journey and stories from those fortunate to have had him as a guide. The abundant stories in his book beautifully and effectively give life to the concepts and approaches that form the core of his important contribution to this new vision. Fruitful Aging is filled with Tom's deep, nature-based spirituality: a spirituality that opens the heart and elevates the mind while being practical and down to earth. If you've done lots of other reading on conscious aging, reading Tom's book will not be redundant. If you are new to this exploration, what an inspiring way to begin!"

—Ron Pevny, Founder and Director of the Center for Conscious Eldering and Coordinator of the Conscious Aging Alliance

"Tom Pinkson has developed a practical and transformative approach to fruitful aging.

Tom has been a valued visionary teacher in the Institute of Noetic Sciences Conscious Aging program series where he was very well received. His insights on ways to focus our intentions and attention in creating a new vision for aging are very potent. I am grateful for Tom's work and am so pleased that his work is now available to all through this book."

—Kathleen Erickson-Freeman, Institute of Noetic Science Elder Education Program Manager

Fruitful Aging

Finding the Gold In
The Golden Years

By

Tom Pinkson

Dedication

This book is dedicated to Guadalupe de la Cruz, my Huichol Native American spiritual grandmother and to my dear friend Don Leonard, who both found gold in the toughest of times. Gratitude to those who share their fruitful stories herein: Janie Rezner, Nancy Corser, Phil Sheridan, Gary Topper, Teddy Olwyler, Jerry Jampolsky, Diane Cirrincione and Mike Lerner. May your gold shine on.

Gratitude to Andrea, my loving and beautiful wife of 46 years, my precious daughters Kimberly and Nicole, my inspirational grandsons Corbin, Luke and Sebastian, and my fine son-in-laws, Justin and Frank, for your love and support no matter what I do.

Gratitude to Brent MacKinnon for huge help throughout the writing of this book, to Susan Cole for invaluable editing and suggestion help, to Roger Clay for his help in formatting and to

Bobby Sarnoff, Angeles Arrien Foundation, Marion Weber, Karen Kustel, Pat and Paul Taylor and Penelope More for your support in allowing me time to do this writing.

Gratitude to my dear sisters, Ilsa and Briane, and their husbands, Pat Burke and Mark Humpal, for your love and support through the years and to the People of Wakan without whose support I would not be who I am.

Gratitude to my mother, Ruth Ester, my father, Fred, my dad, Ray, my grandparents Sarah and Nathan Podolsky and Ella and Benjamin Soloway, for the love you gave me as a child that still blooms in my heart.

Fruitful Aging: Finding the Gold in the Golden Years is about meeting the challenges of aging in a skillful manner using them as vehicles to grow this time of life into the richest and most rewarding time of all.

Table of Contents

Preface

Dr. Tom Herington

In my many years of clinical practice, both as physician and as clinical psychologist, I have observed countless patients and clients confront the challenges of aging. These challenges—physical, psychological, and spiritual—typically impact the very core of our lives in profound, dramatic and unexpected ways.

Our elder years can present us with some tough experiences. Changes in our bodies and minds often feel unwelcome and can leave us struggling as our faculties soften. Things just don't seem to work as fluidly and easily as they used to.

These are tremors that can shake us off our feet, can undermine us at a time when we most need a strong sense of self and well-being in order to meet a radical set of changes to the very structure of our lives. Think about facing the impact of retirement, loss of income, displacement of self-identity, loss of mobility, loss of faculties, loss of home, the merciless onslaught of pain, and the dissolution of relationship and family as our spouses, partners, and loved ones precede us in death. Think about facing these trials without our best self at hand or worse, with a stricken or weary remnant of self.

This topic—aging, and in particular, the experience of one's own personal aging—is not an easy one to engage. Typically we meet aging as best we can, with whatever support and sustenance is or is not available; with whatever tools may or may not be at hand; and with whatever skill we have or do not have at wielding them effectively. Aging is an experience shared by every person on the planet; yet how we think about it, relate to it, navigate it, actually do it, varies tremendously. As you (or someone you know) move into this stage of life, how will it play out for you? Do you have a say in the outcome? What choice is left when so many choices are taken from you? What do you really know about this process and what can you really count on to be of help?

Tom Pinkson's book asks us to consider our readiness for this process as he invites us on a powerful journey of self-reflection and preparation. His very personal and poignant life story commissions us to frame our own. His words engage us in the uniquely individual exploration and reassessment of our own life narrative. His questions and exercises provide practical, useful, and powerful opportunities to prepare ourselves for the destined pilgrimage that we have already undertaken.

Sharing guidance, both from his own experience and from that of other wisdom elders, Tom invites us to deepen our awareness in order to recognize, then to mine, the gold in our own golden years. He calls us to clarify what we mean by gold and to use our own life history as a vehicle to identify what is truly meaningful in our lives. This process helps us create a uniquely personal vision in which meaning supplants emptiness; acceptance befriends submission; and surprisingly, choice appears where none seemed possible.

Fortunately, we are not left with vision alone because Tom also supplies practical tools for achieving it. Much of the book is devoted to specific steps and practices that help us move towards attaining the golden experience of elderhood that we hope for. It is best read with pen and notebook at hand because it engages us and calls us to action so that we can generate a real outcome, that is, a rich, fulfilling, and resilient life.

Importantly, the valuable guidance in this book is presented in a way that lends inspiration to both journey and sojourner alike. As we journey along Tom's path of reassessment, we discover new opportunities to experience personal meaning in life and to explore how this meaning can inform the vision we might hold for living out our elder years. In turn, the sojourner is inspired by Tom's constant reminders of a larger context to life, of our inter-relatedness, and of our integral relationship to a larger universe. He speaks to our common humanity and inspires our better selves to inscribe the final chapters of our lives with values that enrich both ourselves and others.

Be clear that this is not a book of platitudes for seniors. Tom does not deny reality. Rather, he embraces the bewildering, demanding, and overwhelming experience of aging in a manner that reveals to us its hidden meaning, inner richness, and unexpected pleasure. Taking us beyond the notion of mere endurance Tom makes it clear that we can continue to author and live a rich and fulfilling life even as its very structure changes under our feet.

I am grateful for the light that Tom, through this book, shines ahead onto a mysterious path and am grateful for his inspiration to keep moving forward in a good way, one step at a time. I am grateful for the fellowship of walking companions and for good company on the life path. This book is both beacon and companion. It is a book to be read, to learn from, and most importantly, to feel.

Aging and death are multi-faceted and complex. What to do? As Tom says, *"Dream with clear intention for the fullest blossoming of your inner flowers. Then do your best to live it out."* He supports us in clarifying this intention for ourselves and provides the tools for its transformation into the gold of a richly lived, seasoned life.

Tom Herington, MD, PsyD.
Spring 2013

Introduction

Tom Pinkson

We are sacred, worthy, luminous beings.
We are love and our love is for giving.

I don't know about you but I'm getting older. One week after celebrating my 63rd birthday ski touring in a glorious Sierra snowstorm, disaster hit big time. Bending down to move a newly delivered cord of wood from our driveway into the carport, my lower back tightened up. Standing upright brought sharp pain. Uh oh. Major Trouble.

Hobbling into the house I managed to get an ice pack out of the freezer and painfully lay down on the couch. I barely moved until the next morning when I went to see a physical therapist who put me in traction for ten minutes. It felt great. I stood up smiling, *"Wow, that really helped. Thank you so much."*

Relieved, I walked happily to the door. Five steps later the bottom fell out as a volcano exploded in my right hip and left leg. I fell to the floor screaming in agony. A grim faced attendant wheels me to the emergency room of a hospital, which fortunately is right next-door. Unfortunately, it is jammed full with patients filling the hallway. *"We'll get to you as soon as we can,"* says a nurse rushing past with a mangled body on a gurney.

I have no idea how long I lay there in a burning hell of pain. Thank goodness, my wife Andrea arrived. A nurse herself, she begged passing nurses for help. *"I'm so sorry"*, they say as they rush bye. *"We are so busy now. We'll be with you as soon as possible."*

"As soon as possible" turns into an excruciatingly long wait. Sciatic fire burns down my hip, down my left thigh, and into my knee. *"Ahhhhh!"* Freaked out in unbearable pain, I beg for release - *"Please God. I can't take this. Get me out of here. Let me die if that's the only way out. Anything but this. Mercy. Please. Mercy. I can't do this any longer!"*

In these fires of hell a judgmental part of me scornfully comments, *"So this is what it comes down to when the shit hits the fan – you're reduced to pitiful begging."*

Despite my pleas, I didn't die; however, I did fall apart. The pain shot me through some kind of time tunnel. I was in the past with others in pain - friends, relatives, people I knew. I was with both my Dads at the time of their deaths. I was with my 22-year-old uncle Sunny whose plane was shot down in WW II. I was with my lifelong friend Steve, who had died choking from cancer of the esophagus. I was with all the children I had worked with at the Center for Attitudinal Healing over the years dying from cancer. The pain-induced time warp shot me forward in time as well. There I witnessed future scenarios of pain and suffering that could come in my really older years.

My heart dissolved in overwhelming empathy and compassion for everyone suffering in severe pain. Love surged from my heart like water from a broken dam to everyone who ever had been in pain, to everyone who would ever be in pain. *"I'm so sorry. I'm here with you."* My pain remained but the love pouring out of my heart lightened its impact.

After what seemed like an eternity of agony, a nurse finally stopped at my gurney. *"We can take you now,"* she said. *"A doctor can see you"*. She wheeled me through a corridor into another hallway. Gurneys were everywhere. A doctor appeared. Andrea explained what had happened. He gave me a shot of morphine. Blessed Hallelujah. Merciful relief began to flow into my ravaged body.

An MRI revealed one herniated disk, another bulging, L3, and L4, at the base of the spine, causing sciatica down my left side. I was sent home later that day loaded on all kinds of pain medication. I ended up flat on my back for six and a half weeks. Ever try eating on your back? What about lying on your back all day long because that is the only posture you can tolerate without agony? Even then, periodic bursts of searing fire shoot through reducing me to a soaking wet quivering wreck.

Going to the bathroom is a nightmare. The hospital gave me crutches but even with that aid there is too much pressure on my spine to use them. The only way to get there is to lower myself to the ground, then crawl on all four legs like a dog. Once at the commode I have to sit up. The pressure on my back is unbelievable. I struggle to not pass out while doing my business. Miserable doesn't get close to describing it.

In the midst of it all, a gift of grace shines through darkness and despair, an inner voice.

There is an intelligence within you that knows how to heal. There is an intelligence available to you that knows how to heal. Open up to it. Listen to it. Work with it. Open to anything that might be able to help. This is a huge learning time for you. Let go of any thoughts about how long this is going to take. Surrender. You will heal completely if you let go of any timetable and work with the Intelligence.

Jerry Jampolsky, my friend and spiritual elder brother from the Center for Attitudinal Healing (which he founded and with whom I had worked for 32 years), called on my second day home from the hospital. Wracked by pain spasms, spaced out on drugs, I was barely conscious. *"Tom"*, Jerry said, *"it's important that you remember you are not your body, you are not your pain, you are not your ego, your thoughts or even your feelings. You are light. You are love. Close your eye, +"* he said. *"Focus on light. Repeat after me, 'Your infinite light and love is what I see, it is but a reflection of the light and love in me'."*

In a trance-like state, I grab Jerry's words like a drowning man grabs a safety line. I repeat them whenever the pain hits - *"I am not this pain, I am not my body, I am the infinite light and love."* I visualize a flow of healing light entering with the breath. I direct it into my back, my side, my thigh, and my knee. I breathe out, visualizing pain as a dark liquid leaving my body. I ride the pain wave down my leg into the ground. Gradually the intensity begins to lessen. After several minutes I am ok. *"My God, this is Heaven!"*

Heaven is short-lived. All too soon pain roars back. Nights are especially hard. Since I eat on my back, swallowing is difficult. I gag. I remember the panic I felt as a child during an asthma attack. I doze off. Waking with a terror that I will choke to death in my sleep I look at Andrea, who is sleeping by my side, and worry that she will find me dead in the morning.

Short moments of peace come as blessings but they last only until another wave of anxiety, fear and pain rises up to steal my peace. I worry I will never be able to walk again, never ride a bike again, never hike in my beloved nature again.

Over and over I repeat the mantra, *"Your infinite light and love is what I see, it is but a reflection of the infinite light and love in me."*

Andrea, along with my daughters Kimberly and Nicole, are angels of mercy, as are caring friends and work colleagues, who come to visit bringing food, herbs, vitamins, various healing modalities of touch, massage, acupuncture, and their tender love and support. After several bedridden weeks indoors lying on my back wrestling with demons of depression, fear, despair, and reccurring anxiety attacks, I hunger to be outdoors. Fortunately, a sunny, in-the-middle-of-winter week arrives. Sunlight beams into our bedroom. I need out. Andrea is away doing errands. It's up to me. I gingerly lower my body onto the floor, crawl out the doorway and onto the front deck.

I place a pillow under my knees, one under the base of my spine, another under my head. Moving slowly, I carefully lower myself onto my back. Majestic cotton-candy clouds drift across a blue ocean of sky. Warm sunlight is manna from heaven to my nature-starved body and soul. Trees and bushes wave gracefully in a gentle breeze. Two crows rest on an overhead power line chattering away. A blue jay alights on an oak branch. A red-crested hummingbird buzzes by. Everything glows. Compared to where I have been, this is deliverance. Joyful praise to all.

"Thank you powers of nature. Thank you, thank you. Thank you Great Spirit, for this beautiful day." Reveling in it all until the exhaustion of

sleep deprivation, stress and medication overtakes me, my eyelids close. I drift off into reverie.

"What is this pain trying to tell me?" I wonder. *"What is it trying to help me see?"* I damn sure never want to go through this kind of suffering again, so any information this injury might be trying to show me, I want to get! *"Don't protect my ego. I want to see and get whatever I need to see, no holds barred!"*

In dreamlike recall I remember work I had done years before with Dr. Arnold Mindell, author of *Shaman's Body* and founder of a mind/body/ spirit approach to healing he termed *"Process Work"*. Mindell believes unwanted symptoms, disruptions, illness, mistakes and injuries are unconscious parts of us trying to be known. He suggests they are teachers knocking on the door trying to help us become conscious of something important. From Mindell I learned the concept of entering into dialogue with disturbing occurrences using what he terms "second attention" to get their messages.

"Become the block or disturbance," says Mindel. *"Find the symptom-maker. Explore its qualities. Ask, "What is it trying to show me? What can I learn? Trust and unfold what is trying to emerge."*

With plenty of down time and nothing to lose I give his techniques a go. Closing my eyes, I direct awareness into the pain. Images appear. I see a burning hot lava rock lodged in the herniated disk. Looking deeper I see it is a storehouse of pain and anger going back to the wounded child whose father died two months before his fourth birthday.

Another image appears in the contracted muscles surrounding the herniated disk. It is a large metal vice squeezing my back and knee along with a shadowy figure, the *"pain-maker,"* smashing a sharp metal chisel into another red-hot lava rock. Each smash shoots an excruciating lighting strike into my lower back, thigh, knee and calf. In this moment I see my lifelong reactive pattern of lashing-out blame and anger when frustrated coming from the *"pain-maker"* who under ordinary circumstances hides in dark shadows until activated.

Despite years of healing work to get in touch with a gentler, feminine part of my psyche and self, I now see there is an unconscious retention of this pattern operating in my life that causes unwarranted tension, tightness and reactivity. The pattern began in adolescence when I entered junior high school as an eleven year old, the youngest in the school with guys 15, 16, even 17 in the ninth grade. It was a tough school, fights in the hallway on a regular basis. My first week a ninth-grader pulled a knife threatening a teacher. I was terrified. It seemed to me my only hope of surviving this nightmare was to develop enough physical strength, toughness and the threat of violence that people would leave me alone. It all came from fear. I asked for weights as a birthday present. I worked out like a maniac, taking food supplements that promised to help me grow big muscles. My strategy worked. By the age of 15 I was bigger, stronger, and tougher. After a few fights I earned a reputation as a *"bad guy"*; I was left alone.

As an adult I no longer physically acted violent but an energetic pattern of automatically trying to use force when frustrated still existed deep inside. Like termite rot in the basement of a house, I recognized it had to go if I wanted real healing. I saw how the burning sciatic pain erupted from a normally dormant volcano located in the base of the spine, my backbone, and my foundation. I saw how the volcano activated when frustration reared its head. Then, an attacking energy force roared out to do battle causing undue stress and strain on others in addition to myself.

I began dialoging with the pain-maker by sending questions into it, then watching what came back in response. Slowly I began to realize my back injury was a gift, not something bad but an emergency call. If I kept my old pattern going it would shorten my life and make the time I did have considerably less pleasant. The fear-based strategy of force and attack needed to go. I needed a new way of being. Lying there on our deck in the sunshine I heard a quiet inner voice:

Use the opening of the herniated disk to clean out the toxic energy of the old pattern. Breathe it out. Let it go. Bring in a different energy through the opening.

There was more.

Face your challenges with 'faith muscle', not force muscle. Trust the intelligence that knows how to heal you is present all the time. Surrender to the light that has been helping you through the pain spasms. It transforms pain into love. Surrender into the light that you are.

Shift your focus from fearful ego to the transformational power of light. That's your true source of strength and security, not physical muscles or anything of the physical world.

Be patient. Trust that you will be completely healed just not on your timetable. It will be on divine time. Don't try to force anything. Healing will happen as you allow it to happen. Do your part – work that faith muscle. Stay with the light. Let the old pattern die. Release into bigger currents. Trust the intelligence. It's been around for a long time. It knows.

Grateful and buoyed in spirit but worn out emotionally, I lacked confidence in meeting the challenge. I felt alone, small, and weak. I could see a chorus of *"poor me"* starting to warm up. Suddenly a loud shriek from the sky jolted me awake. I looked up. A red tail hawk circled directly above me, its tail feathers shining brilliantly in the sunlight.

In previous experiences with red tail hawks while hiking, I'd marvel at their huge looping flight paths. This hawk was different. It stayed and stayed, circling slowly above. I watched in awe and amazement. The hawk sent a message telepathically — *"You are not alone. Larger currents are in operation and you are a part of it, right now and always, including this injury and your entire life - past, present and future! Release into bigger currents! Release. Release!"*

Some part of me left my body there on the deck to merge with the soaring hawk. Looking down I saw my suffering body. From this heightened perspective it dawned on me how the suffering, infirmity, pain, helplessness and dependency on others served as a preview of the challenges aging can bring – loss of independence, loss of functionality, and total reliance on others to meet basic needs. Slowly it dawned in my mind that my injury was experiential learning into what it's like to live with an age-ravaged body that no longer does what you want it to, exactly what many older people have to deal with every day.

"Wow! What interesting timing," I thought to myself. *"Two weeks after starting my group on conscious aging I get a direct experience about what can happen as you age, how devastating and overwhelming it feels when you can't get around like you used to."* Thankful for this new understanding, I appreciated even more the incredible importance

of loving care and support I had received from my family and friends.

I was also thankful for learning the most helpful thing I could do in dealing with pain was surrendering in faith and trust to the presence of light and love. Slow, conscious breathing, opening to larger presence, releasing fear or judgment thoughts that closed my heart, repeating my mantra, connecting with the love-essence of my being was the winning formula. Sending love-light out to others brought peace. It didn't magically make the pain disappear overnight, but it helped lessen its severity. This brought blessed relief restoring confidence that I would come out the other side of this experience better than when I entered, so long as I learned the lessons and did the inner work.

Tearful gratitude flowed. I sent a silent message to the circling hawk. *"Thank you Hawk Spirit. Thank you for coming to me. Thank you Great Spirit, for sending this sign I am not alone. You are with me."*

The healing process deepened my surrender work releasing with faith and trust into the embodied cosmic intelligence that knows how to heal injured bodies. It's the same cosmic intelligence that brought a warm sunny day in the heart of winter that brought a circling hawk when I felt overwhelmed. I watched my consciousness move from victim state *"poor me"* to a spiritually empowered state recognizing gifts of grace in troublesome situations.

My back injury served as a test and opportunity to strengthen my faith muscle: to trust a *"larger, higher presence,"* God, Spirit, and the Mystery. The pain and suffering weren't about punishment, they were about helping me grow spiritually.

Six consecutive days of sunny weather allowed me to crawl out on the deck every afternoon. To my total amazement and delight, a hawk joined me each day. On the fourth day another red tail showed up. Twice as good! They circled together, soaring majestically higher, then descending, then higher, and then descending, always directly above. I couldn't believe it. I called Andrea to come out and witness it.

More gratitude: *"Thank you Great Spirit. Thank you for sending these beautiful hawks. Thank you for helping me in ways I do not fully understand but which I welcome. Thank you, Hawk Spirits. Thank you for your lives. Please carry my love to others who need it for their healing. Thank you so much for your precious gifts."*

The two hawks flew again on the fifth and sixth day. On the seventh day they came again. I lay in awe marveling at my good fortune. Out of nowhere a peregrine falcon swooshed five feet over my head! *"Unbelievable! My tingling bones knew instantly this was affirmation and reward for my work with surrender. The trust was right on target!"*

Winter returned the next day. My outdoor sojourn with the hawks was over. Shortly thereafter the doctor said I could start hydrotherapy. Family and friends took turns driving me to a nearby health club. I wobbled over to the car on crutches, carefully lying down on the back seat with pillows to avoid pressure on my spine. I still couldn't sit up. I prayed we wouldn't hit any bumps.

Hydrotherapy took place in a large heated pool with participants ranging in age from late sixties to over a hundred. It was a community of elders who'd been doing therapy together for some time, each person trying to make the best of a hard situation. There was a wonderful camaraderie amongst them, a great deal of joking, laughter and caring support. I was the youngest one there. They warmly welcomed me into their club.

To be amongst such encouraging models of conscious aging was truly a gift for me. I loved how they showed up each day, some in wheelchairs, with walkers, some paralyzed, but always exploring what was possible and doing that with good cheer and determination.

Floating in the warm water with weights on my ankles provided traction, while an inner tube under my arms held me up. No pressure on my backbone, upright, no pain for the first time in over a month. Pure bliss.

Hydrotherapy worked wonders. So did the cumulative effects of the many alternative treatment modalities offered by friends, along with the devoted love and care from Andrea and my daughters. Slowly but surely the pain lessened, my back grew stronger. Two months after starting hydrotherapy I returned to work. Winter rolled into spring, with new life coming up from the earth's blossoming buds and transforming into flowers, bees buzzing and birds singing. There was new life in me too. I loved it!

Fortunately, over several months of bed-rest and more months of therapy I recovered full mobility and returned to the routines of my life. Seven months later I hoisted a 45-pound backpack to lead my annual 6-day vision quest retreat in the High Sierra. I had a minor backache when I took my pack off that night, but I sent love to my back and with a few days' rest and some Advil, I was fine. Hallelujah! The intelligence that knows how to heal had done its work.

During my fasting solitude-time on quest I reflected on how my healing journey helped me see longevity's greatest gift is the opportunity it provides to grow spirituality. I felt huge gratitude for the regenerative healing wisdom living in our bodies, which nature shows us in her many manifestations. We truly are part of *"larger and bigger currents."*

More than ever I now realized how we are so much more than our bodies. As amazing as they are, bodies are temporary containers for our light-filled spirits to live in during our time on Earth. Our egos are the identities we form in relationship to our bodies and their life experiences, but truth be told, we are so much more than bodies, than thoughts, than ego-based identity. In our deepest depths we are luminous light beings here to wake up and remember our essence is love and that this love, which we are, is for giving.

Years later my back is fine so long as I stay

vigilant with conscious movement, conscious lifting, and conscious gratitude. I had to accept I have a vulnerability that demands attention and respect. As a result I do daily core strengthening and stretching exercise. Now, just knowing that I am a work in progress supports me in each new day to live a *faith-filled flow*. This strategy for life replaces the old one, the fear-based force that had been unconsciously running my life.

"No more," I vowed. *"I get it. I don't want to ever return to that kind of pain again. From now on I listen to any 'take-it-easy-message' I get. No more forcing, no more pushing. Let go. Surrender. Stop and rest when needed, send love, relax, get a massage. Trust the intelligence that knows how to heal."*

My journey of recovery had elements of an intense personal growth retreat. Yoga and meditation techniques learned during my undergraduate years at San Francisco State in the mid-'60's, along with attitudinal healing, visualization practices, gratitude, prayer and inner dialogue work brought healing. Thus, I was able to mine precious gold from what could have been just a very depressing time on every level. I hope to have a good run of many more years to enjoy that gold and mine even more but there is no guarantee of even tomorrow.

The back injury that had plunged me into a total dependence upon others when I was no longer able to walk, sit or stand on my own had also, in effect, catapulted me forward in time. It gave me a preview of what it might be like to be an incapacitated older man, no longer able to contribute, no longer able to do anything except lie on my back suffering in despair, feeling useless, worthless, depressed, anxious and a burden on others. As my denial system shattered I became fearful of what the future could hold.

Realistically, I wanted to look at the potential challenges. I wanted to learn how to use those challenges as opportunities to grow into my fullest creative potential on all levels of being - physical, emotional, intellectual and spiritual. I wanted to know what I could do that offered the best chance of making whatever years I had left the richest and most meaningful ones of my entire life. A tall order but that was my goal.

Pouring over the latest scientific research on all aspects of growing older I learned about neuro-plasticity: the brain's ability to create new brain cells at any age. I read books, journals, websites and blogs about conscious aging. I interviewed older people I knew and respected who were living rich lives. I reflected on my own rite of passage experiences with indigenous peoples around the world, my forty years of vision questing in the Sierra Mountains of California and my shamanic explorations of consciousness expansion and mysticism with psychedelics, meditation, yoga, long-distance running, mountain climbing and prayer, as well as Eastern and Western religions. I reviewed what I had learned from almost half a century pursuing the techniques, tools and philosophies of the full panoply of the human potential movement. I read back over my writings from working with life-threatened and terminally ill patients through the many years of my practice as a psychologist.

This book shares the results of my process, research and reflection. It brings an empowered vision of what the final stanza of life can be: an adventurous exploration of possibility, making it the juiciest time of all.

In working clinically with hundreds of individuals and groups, I see that aging fruitfully with happiness, wellbeing, and fulfillment requires addressing Five Developmental Challenges of the second half of life. Each challenge builds on and informs the next.

The Five Developmental Challenges are:

1. **REVISION** – Your mortality to create an ally relationship that empowers living.

2. **RECLAIM & REPAIR** – Wisdom of your life through a *"Harvesting Review Process"* that taps into the power of love to heal wounded relationships.

    Healing your Relationships

3. **REALIZE** – The Vision and Purpose of your Heart Path Mission & Live Your Legacy.

4. **REAWAKEN** – Creativity and courage to generate meaningful self-expression and service in the world.

5. **REALIZE** –Your highest potential by growing your spiritual maturity and intelligence.

These five developmental challenges reach completion in a transitional rite that crosses the threshold into fruitful aging. Toward this end I developed a program called *Recognition Rites Honoring Elders*, which supports a shift of negative attitudes and perceptions about the process of aging into positive ones. Special emphasis is given to an innate drive in the elder years toward what is now called *gero-transcendence* — the spiritual drive towards realizing oneness with the divine.

This book is an invitation to see what these ideas spark in you using your gift of longevity and its challenges as a vehicle towards the most fruitful blossoming of your selfhood, your creative expression, your wisdom lessons, and your love in a world that so desperately needs more love. One suggestion before proceeding; get a journal that you keep at your side while reading this book. There will be thoughts, insights, reflections, ideas and inspirations rising up in your mind that you want to catch. They are light rays that will illuminate your path.

This book also brings an invitation to live the remaining years of your life so when the end comes, you can look back with full satisfaction knowing you completed what you came here to do. Then you can leave with a smile in your soul and a heart full of gratitude for the fulfilling time you had being here. The Hawaiian language has a word, *"pohala,"* which has dual meanings. One refers to the regaining of consciousness. The other meaning is *"to open as flower petals."*

My prayer is that reading this book may help you open the petals of your consciousness to the truth of who and what you are, a sacred worthy luminous golden being of love. May it be so!

Chapter One

The One Who Loves the Most Wins

A silver tsunami of increasing longevity is sweeping across the nation. Over the next several decades, the number of Americans over age 60 will increase by nearly 70 percent, the largest increase for any age group in the population. (Annual Conference of the American Society on Aging 2011). Aging is happening not just with us humans but also with everything born, from galaxies to mountains to humans. Everything ages over time, eventually winds down, and dissolves away. It is a natural process that doesn't require agreement, knowledge or planning. The issue is not about whether aging happens, it does. The issue is how it will happen for you. Will it be positive? Fulfilling? Meaningful?

Will it be fruitful, the time of your greatest blossoming, the experiencing of your greatest good? Or will it be an unhappy time shaped by harmful attitudes and beliefs conditioned by our society's negative attitudes towards aging and older people? Will you fall victim to the challenges of aging — especially those of change, loss and the inevitability of personal mortality? Or do you have a repertoire of practical knowledge, tools and skill sets to use in successfully embracing all the life and vitality of your remaining years?

If so, good for you. Go get 'em! But if not, this book will help you, or someone special you know in their sixties, their seventies, their eighties and beyond to find the real gold in what has been loosely referred to as the *Golden Years*.

What is the gold of life for you? Is it the literal gold of material success and reward? Is it prestige, status, accomplishment? What truly opens your heart and brings you the most joy, the most satisfaction, the most meaning? Several years ago at a friend's house I noticed a card tacked on his wall that really hit home. It read, *"In the game of life, the one who loves the most wins!"* I don't necessarily think of life as a game but I do know in my 68 years on the planet, the richest experiences of my life have all had something to do with loving and feeling loved, with giving love and receiving love. Sometimes it was with another person, sometimes it was with nature, and sometimes it was with myself. Sometimes it was with the luminous presence of spirit.

Feeling loved and loving helps me feel secure, peaceful, joyful, confident, strong and full of wellbeing. I like that. That is the state I want to experience more frequently, more consistently. Like the saying on the wall, I call that winning.

That is the real gold, the preciousness of life lived with open heart.

It seems I am not alone in my thoughts on what constitutes the real gold in life. Scientific evidence identifies the importance of meaning and purpose toward healthy aging. Meaning has to do with purpose and belonging. (*Buddha's Brain: The Practical Neuroscience of Happiness, Love and Wisdom*. Rick Hanson). Beyond the physical needs of food, shelter and touch, our greatest needs as human beings are about supportive connection, acceptance and contribution with others, with the animating powers of nature and with the universe that give us life. Then we can act with integrity, faith, and trust, tapping our creativity in ways that provide satisfaction and joy.

Discovering a sense of purpose has deep meaning, an awareness of belonging as well as feeling connected to something larger than the individual self that is ultimately about love. Witness the fact that people who belong to a church or spiritual group or who have an active spiritual life live, on average, seven years longer than those who don't. (Koenig – *Handbook of Religion and Health* 2001).

I was fortunate in my early years to be born to two parents who loved me and showed it in many ways. There were never doubts that I was loveable and loved. What a gift. My troubles started when I was devastated by my dad's death a few months before my fourth birthday. My mother was hospitalized for emergency surgery on her thyroid. My ten-month old sister and I were shuttled from one aunt's house to another aunt's house for the six weeks she was in the hospital. No one knew how to help a youngster deal with loss in those days of the late 1940's. My grief was bottled up inside, which led to life-threatening asthma attacks that continued into my teen years.

The arrival of testosterone at adolescence exploded the unresolved grief into acting-out juvenile delinquency, drug abuse, violence and crime that, were it not for the protection and grace of something greater than I, this book wouldn't be written because I would be dead or in jail. It was all about the loss of love, a teaching about impermanence that I was too young to integrate at the time, in part because no one was around who knew how to help me do so.

So while I knew about the goodness of love in my most formative years, I also knew about the pain of its loss. Yet I couldn't articulate it at the time. Gradually a question arose that school and conventional society of the 1950's did not come close to addressing – *"In a world where death has the power to come at any time and take a loved one without needing our permission, what, if anything, is living a life based on?"*

That question eventually took me around the world exploring the life-ways of indigenous peoples of different cultures since I wasn't finding answers that spoke to me with any sense of truth, power or meaning in my own culture. In an earlier book, *The Shamanic Wisdom of The*

Huichol: Medicine Teachings For Modern Times, I wrote about that journey in depth. Here I refer to that cycle of my life as a motivating factor for a lifelong exploration for what truly matters the most in life. Was it all just a cruel joke, a set-up for disappointment, given that love could vanish in an instant? What's the point, why invest at all? Why open to love if you are just going to be torn asunder when it leaves?

Beginning this existential journey I was a confirmed, cynical, pessimistic, bitter atheist. Religion was the opiate of the masses, a denial system for those too weak to face the reality of death and the injustices and traumas of life. A life-changing luminous experience with LSD in my early twenties blew out the fuse-box of my entire belief system. It showed me an entirely different understanding of reality. It also blew out the full weight of my grief, pain and sadness from unresolved loss that had been previously repressed, somatasized, and then acted out through alcohol-fueled violence on people and property. I wailed like a wounded animal.

At the time I was an honors psychology undergraduate, a political and social justice activist protesting the war in Vietnam and volunteering in a tutorial program with inner city disadvantaged youth.

The mind fascinated me. I wanted to understand more about the acting-out delinquency of my teenage years. I was fascinated but frightened by the reports I was hearing about this new, then legal substance, LSD that was being used in research projects to open access to the deeper reaches of the unconscious. After a year of preparation and with trusted guides, I went ahead and took the plunge.

The LSD expanded my consciousness into union with the underlying spiritual essence of ultimate reality as well as the healing transformational presence and power of infinite unconditional love, the true gold of existence. The same information came through again fifteen years later sitting around a ceremonial fire in the desert wilderness of backcountry Mexico with Huichol Indians. It came through repeatedly from three decades from helping start the first at-home hospice in the United States, and then with the Center for Attitudinal Healing in Marin County, California, sitting bedside with terminally ill children and adults. When pain, fear, suffering and death came calling, it was only love, peace and faith that held any currency of meaning. Everything else fell by the wayside.

Essence of our Being

Through these door-openings I learned the very essence of our being is love: it is who and what we actually are. We are so much more than our bodies, so much more than our ego identity with all its history and stories. We are more than our thoughts, our feelings, our sensations, even more than our minds in their ordinary state of consciousness that is based on perceptions of separation. I saw that on the deepest levels of our being we are all, always, connected. Interconnected actually, in an invisible web that is of infinite measure. The energy of this web is what we call love.

When we open to it, the pain of separation dissolves. When we close off to it through thought-forms of guilt, shame, limitation, negative judgments about our own being or the being of others, as distinguished from judging behavior, the heart closes, thrusting us into an imprisonment of contraction, fear and dis-ease. When we have had enough suffering and choose anew to release the pain-causing thoughts, not repress or deny or project, but release and let go, the heart reopens to the transformational healing power of love. This love is not something we create. It is a gift of grace, like the breath, given to us by the creative wisdom power of the universe, whatever you are comfortable calling it – Father God, Mother Goddess, Holy Spirit, Yahweh, Shekinah, Great Spirit, Allah, Great Mystery, Nature, Creator, Higher Power, Cosmic Consciousness or as some sub-atomic physicists refer to it, an infinite field of *"cosmic foam."*

Love lives in all of us and each of us has the gift of free choice: whether to open to, honor, attune with and nurture the love, or not. I don't believe there is a right or wrong choice here, just the reality that whatever choice we make will bear different results in the quality of our life experience. The choice is ours. Many studies demonstrate that the heart is an exceptionally keen organ of perception, sending messages, warnings, and information of all kinds before the brain responds. The main information it sends is the always present gift of unconditional love – who and what we are.

I don't know about you but I have had enough suffering over the years. I certainly don't want to create more through using my mind unskillfully by closing it off to the presence of love. I want to use the gift of choice that comes in with each breath to do whatever I can do to open my awareness to love's presence. Children I worked with at the Center for Attitudinal Healing call this being a *"love-giver"* and a *"love-finder"*: that is setting your intention on opening the heart and sending love to self and others instead of trying to get love back from someone or trying to control or manipulate a situation. You can always find something to criticize in someone if this is your goal, but you can also choose to look beneath his or her lampshade for their light. Look for the love; perhaps it is hidden beneath fear or acting out behaviors.

The idea is that our essence is love so in any given moment we are either giving love or asking for it. Sometimes, out of ignorance or as a result of our wounds, we ask for it in unskillful ways, leaving us frustrated because we don't get what we want. Know that we already have it, right down in our hearts. If we only knew that love doesn't die, bodies do, but love doesn't. Relationships continue in our hearts and our minds if we let them, if we honor our grief in healthy ways but also stay open to connection in our hearts.

Choosing to open to love's presence in turn opens the door to experiencing a conscious communion of connection that transcends time and space into a deeply felt, positive sense of the sacred, the real gold of life.

Chapter Two

REVISION: Death as an Ally

What did your face look like
before you were born?

—Zen Koan

The first developmental challenge, befriending mortality into an ally or *helper* relationship that stimulates full-force living, may be the toughest to face. Death, especially our own, is something that most of us deliberately try not to think about; it's just too upsetting. You may want to go on to the next chapter and then come back to this one when you feel ready. You have a choice.

I didn't have a choice in the matter however as death burst into my life at the age of three and a half years when my Dad died. It was a hard and sorrowful introduction to the existence of a force that can take away our loved ones at any time and doesn't need permission to do so.

My awareness of life's fragility and impermanence was shattering. It took many years and hard work to extract something positive out of the traumatic event of my father's death that had so shaped my childhood. After making my way through life-threatening asthma as a youth and juvenile delinquency as a teenager I ended up on a career path in psychology during which time I co-founded the first at-home Hospice Program in the United States. This grew into working with children and adults with life-threatening illness for thirty-two years. (*"Do They Celebrate Christmas in Heaven? Teachings from Children with Life-Threatening Illness"*, Tom Pinkson).

During this time I repeatedly witnessed people not living authentic lives, not living from the soul or from the heart until the time that awareness of their own personal mortality appeared in their lives. Prior to that, a busy, making-ends-meet life style with its many distractions resulted in a thought pattern that said, *"I don't have to do — (fill in whatever you want here). "I don't have to be real, apologize, forgive, open to love, go for what really calls me, etc., until tomorrow, next week, next year, when the moon is in Sagittarius"* or whatever. We put off and postpone authentic living until sometime in the future when conditions are more favorable, thus living half-baked lives of dissatisfaction and frustration.

It doesn't have to be this way. Indigenous author Martin Prechtel calls for a very different response, a confrontive one, which he sees as a spiritual wrestling match: *"Face your own death and face up to the notion you will not live forever,"* says Prechtel.

The value of this kind of confrontation is evidenced in the research from a ten-year study of near-death experiences by Dutch cardiologist Pim van Lommel. He found that nearly every near-death experience involves a life review during which people gain insight into the consequences of their actions. Van Lommel, in his book *"Consciousness Beyond Life: The Science of the Near-Death Experience,"* reports that the experience changes peoples' values.

"They see that life is not about power, appearance, nice cars, clothes, and a young body. It's about entirely different things: love for yourself, nature and your fellow human beings" with an emphasis on trying to *"live more compassionate lives in recognition of the importance of maintaining healthy, caring relationships with those around us."*

In recognition of this finding, my question is — *Why wait to make these life-enhancing changes? Why not take the bull by the horns? Why not create relationship with your death that enhances living by skillfully facing it,* by what mystics refer to as *"dying before dying?"* No matter what denial system you may have in place, in reality death is a constant companion, *"just over your shoulder,"* always present and able to take you out whenever it wants to do so.

One way to befriend your death is to use your

imagination and invite it to come visit you. See and feel what it looks like. Enter into dialogue.

Death asks:

"Do you feel good about how you lived your life?

Where do you find your greatest purpose and meaning, your highest contribution, your greatest accomplishment?

What about your biggest failure?

Do you have any regrets or unfinished business with people or situations?

Anything you would you do differently?

If I took you today, how do you feel about the legacy you leave behind?"

*****

There was a time when I not only didn't know if I'd have a tomorrow, I didn't know if I'd have another moment! It was 1981, a week after I had returned from backcountry Mexico, my first time staying with the Huichol Indians. During my stay I drank contaminated water. As I stood in front of my car about to leave for work my whole body starting violently shaking. Stumbling down the stairs to our front door, I made it five feet into the kitchen where my wife and daughters were just finishing breakfast. I couldn't stop shaking. At first they all thought I was joking around. Andrea, my wife and a pediatric nurse, saw my ashen face. Rushing to my side she felt my forehead. *"My God, you're burning up!"* She took my temperature. It was 106 degrees! *"We're going to the emergency room right now!"*

Somehow the three of them got me back up the stairs and into the car. I don't remember much about the ride but when we got there, an E.R. doctor immediately put me on a gurney, took my temperature and drew some blood. Half delirious I loudly started singing a favorite song — *"Oh Great Spirit, I am calling on you."* Later my wife and I laughed about what this provoked for her because she thought I sang, *"Oh Great Spirit, I'm coming to you!"*

Meanwhile my body was on fire, shaking so hard two nurses had to stand next to me so I wouldn't fall off the gurney. The doctor came back with my blood test results showing a hugely elevated white blood cell count trying to combat a systemic infection whose cause they couldn't determine. They packed me in ice to lower my body temperature, filled me up with all kinds of antibiotics and stood by to see what happened next. I have no idea how long I stayed there singing and shaking, shaking and singing but eventually my temperature began to lower. After several hours they sent me home with more antibiotics and a warning — if my temperature began to rise over 105 degrees, return immediately to the hospital.

For two days I lay shaking in bed alternately freezing and shivering, then burning up and soaking wet in sweat. Andrea reported the doctors still could not pin down what was causing my ordeal but to keep taking the medicine and hope for the best. Every breath was a struggle. When each breath left I didn't know if there would be another one. Death sat on my chest. *"Am I going to die here? Is one of these breaths going to be my last one?"* I didn't know. It sure seemed possible.

All I knew was that when a breath did come in, I was still alive. So I started saying, *"God loves now!"* figuring that if God didn't love now there would be no now and I wouldn't be here so that must mean God loves me too. So with each breath out I started to say, *"Love God now."* Giving thanks. Those two phrases became my mantra. I saw that it was the very bare bones underlying my many years-long practice of yoga, prayers, meditation and spiritual work. It was all I could do. I figured that if I did die, if my spirit did leave on one of the out-breaths, I couldn't go wrong by focusing my attention on loving God, like Gandhi did when he was shot, calling out God's name as he fell to the ground mortally wounded.

Two days later the fever broke, the shaking stopped. Totally weakened and spent from my ordeal, I was relieved to have survived. Hallelujah! Gratitude for healing, for my breath mantra that helped me make it through an initiation of hellfire, a purifying flame that left me both humbled yet stronger and enriched as well. How? I emerged feeling more comfortable with death. I was immensely more aware with presence and gratitude for the preciousness of each moment. Death served as an ally waking me up to life!

Another time of befriending death took place

doing a winter ski tour on Mt. Lassen in Northern California when I got caught in a blizzard with a group of fellow mountaineers. At a certain point in our retreat back to our cars we had to cross a treacherous avalanche zone. We determined that one person at a time would traverse the steep cliff going slowly and softly to avoid setting off a disturbance that could bring the masses of snow above thundering down on our precarious perch. The others stood back in readiness should an avalanche sweep the skier away for their job would be to find and dig the buried person out as soon as it was safe to venture forth.

When my time came, I pushed one foot after the other knowing full well I could be swept away with each footstep possibly being my last. It felt like an eternity with death looming above me at every moment. I never felt so alive or relieved as when I got out of the danger zone. It is truly amazing how facing the possibility of dying at any moment radically enhances awareness of the fragility and preciousness of life. Bottom line; be present for now, all we ever have! Find a way to enjoy it for there is no guarantee of another breath when this one leaves your body.

One other death-befriending experience took place on a white-water raft trip on the Tuolumne River of Yosemite. At the most treacherous part of the run our raft went over a waterfall the wrong way, catapulting me into a raging whirlpool of foaming chaos. It instantly sucked me down into its violent dark depths. Like a mad washing machine it churned me up and down. Thrashing madly and gasping for breath I thought my life was over. After what seemed like another eternity the washing machine spit me back into the main current of the river. I broke the surface with huge relief and made my exhausted way to shore where I collapsed on the bank like a beached whale.

That night, around the campfire the river guides told us that the next day was even more challenging. Terror gripped me in its icy clutch. I felt certain I would be sucked into another whirlpool only this time I would not get out, a reccurring nightmare dream from childhood but now about to come true! My fate was to drown, to never see my wife Andrea again, and to never see my two young daughters grow up.

I stayed up most of the night trying to rid myself of this premonition but it wouldn't budge. There was no respite. No way out. It was only when I finally accepted the mortality that my premonition made so clear that, surprisingly, I was able to get some sleep just before dawn. I determined that if death were to take me the next day on the river I would fight for life with every ounce of strength that I had and that if I lost the battle, at least death would know it didn't win without a huge fight. I awoke a few hours later still fearful but enlivened to meet the challenge. Wouldn't you know, that day on the river went smoothly without a single mishap. My love of life, of being alive expanded exponentially! Facing and befriending mortality works.

But rest assured, you don't have to cross an avalanche zone or go over a waterfall to befriend your death and enrich your living. Follow your awareness inside your body. .Slow down your breathing. Quiet your mind. Focus attention on your heart. It's working for you 24/7 pumping life force through your body. Rest in the moment. It is the only time you are guaranteed, right now, the only time you can experience whatever you want to experience. Examine your deepest values. Is there any greater treasure than love?

Feel and imagine love as an energy of unconditional presence, an invisible, infinite field of light. Choose to visualize love flowing in with each new intake of oxygen. Be totally present for the life giving breath flowing over your lips and into your nose.

Breathe love into our heart and watch it expand, growing brighter with each successive breath. Let it expand out from your heart and into your body, flowing exactly to the places it most needs to go. Breathe peace, surrender and letting-go messages into your muscles. Breathe out fear, tension, judgment, pain, and all thinking that causes stress and tension. Let them go. Use death as an ally. Let them die. Let the energy of love bathe your mind and entire being.

Send some of that love energy out to whom ever comes into your awareness. Buddhists call this *"metta practice"* – extending unconditional loving kindness to self or others. Love energy doesn't stop with walls, nor is it confined by time and space. Affirm to yourself, *"I am a sacred, worthy, luminous being and I am love and my love is for giving."* Allow yourself to notice how you feel when you send unconditional love to yourself and to others, love that has no strings and wants nothing back. You may be surprised at the power of this simple seeming act that can have such profound consequences.

Another way to enrich your living is to befriend your death in the way that shamanic author Carlos Castaneda suggests.

"Death", he says, *"is the only adviser that we ever have. Whenever you feel that everything is going wrong and you're about to be annihilated, turn to your death and ask if that is so. Your death will tell you that you're wrong; that nothing really matters outside its touch. Your death will tell you – 'I haven't touched you yet'."* (Journey to Ixtlan, Carlos Castaneda.)

In my own experience of creating an ally relationship with my death I find it helpful to use the practice Castaneda suggests. I envision the entity of death sitting just over my left shoulder, willing and able to come take my life whenever and however it wants. But rather than having a fearful response to this, I use it to help me be as present as I can be in whatever I am doing and with whomever I am with at the moment.

I silently recite to myself — *"This may be the last thing you ever do in this life. You may never see this person again. You may never do this act again. This may be your 'last dance', so do it with full presence, full awareness. Do it as best you can. Take it all in, and finally, find a way to enjoy it, even if the task is unpleasant, like starting the day cleaning up a stinky mess of foul-looking garbage after the raccoons overturned the trash can in the middle of the night."*

In other words, if I choose to do an ordinarily undesirable action, I find a way to do it that allows me to discover something to be grateful for in the doing of it. Like finding something to be thankful for in the midst of picking up the trash. *"Ok, if I were blind, I couldn't even see this trash so I am glad that my eyes work. I am glad that my arms and legs work so that I can walk, that my nervous system works. I am glad that I have enough money to buy food whose waste becomes trash, to live in a house, to afford to pay for garbage pick-up."* And so on.

This kind of thinking shifts my mental and emotional state from an angry, frustrated, *'poor me'* victim of the circumstances to an enjoyable place of gratitude for the *gifts of the ordinary* so often taken for granted. Living fully in the moment, enjoying now. Death as an ally.

My friends Jerry Jampolsky, 86, and Diane Cirrincione, 68, are spiritual teachers, who turned death into an ally in their quest to fully embody love in their lives. Here's how.

Jerry — *"When we are stuck in our ego mind, bombarded by advertisements of how our bodies should always look beautiful and young, aging becomes an enemy. We become fearful of dying.*

21

We count our aging wrinkles. Aging does not seem like the Golden Age that was promised.

Diane and Jerry

Aging ego-minds make the aging body an enemy, are overly sensitive to rejection, complain a lot, hold grudges and guilt, and think that peace of mind and happiness is not for them.

The fruitful mind is patient, kind, accepting, and full of love, grace and forgiveness. It is not focused on the body, but on giving love away to others, staying away from judging, guilt and grievances. It is curious about life, maintains a sense of humor despite a troublesome outside, and does not believe its true identity is a body, does not believe that the body dying is the end of life.

Regardless of what age we are, our daily

challenges are letting go of our attachments to things in the outside world as the basis for our happiness. I, Jerry, have an enlarged prostate that gets me up to urinate 3 or 4 times a night. This was a challenge at first, but I learned to accept it and not let it interfere with my inner peace. I also have glaucoma, am legally blind in the left eye, can no longer drive, and have night blindness. This bugged me at first but again I learned to accept it and to count my blessings."

Diane adds, *"Both of our biggest challenges are life-long ones — to remember a loving God and to stay in the present, listening carefully to the inner voice of love directing us in what to think, say and do."*

Jerry and Diane start their mornings by preparing themselves to address their challenge. *"We wake up at 4:30am, do some prayers, shower, get dressed and meditate by candlelight every morning. A Course in Miracles has been our heartbeat. It's about self-healing and focuses on practical spirituality and living a life devoted to unconditional love and forgiveness, learning not to withhold our love from anyone, including ourselves.*

"In our aging process we believe forgiveness is as important as breathing so we can be messengers of love and kindness. The most important thing that has taken place for us as we age is having God come first in our relationship. Every day we ask for direction from God on what to think, say and do.

We take one day at a time and when we awake each morning, we affirm to ourselves and each other that this day is going to be the happiest day of our lives, regardless of what is put on our plate."

*****

Hospice physician Dr. Scott Eberle adds his voice to befriending death as a life ally, noting the importance of how rites of passage in indigenous cultures guide initiates through transitions in the life cycle with wisdom teachings on how to live well and how to die well. A key dynamic in all passage rites involves entry into non-ordinary states of consciousness, for this is of vital importance when approaching physical death. The dying process itself often elicits altered states of consciousness, which can be frightening and disorienting if you have no previous experience charting the territory and learning some navigational tools.

When who we think we are in ordinary consciousness is based on ego identification with the physical body, it can be very scary to suddenly be plunged into an altered state by the physiological processes of dying and treatment drugs. You think you are losing your mind and going crazy. If you are fortunate to have experienced an expanded state of consciousness that revealed a deeper level of identity than ego and body, you might *"understand that the physical organism is merely the shell, the rented apartment,"* as spiritual teacher Ram Dass points out.

Rest assured, you don't have to take a psychedelic substance to induce an expanded or numinous state. We have all had them but perhaps not recognized them as such. Observing the birth of a child, witnessing a beautiful sunset, a radiant rainbow's shimmering light, any experience where time seems to stand still and you are caught up in the moment of rapture, joy and bliss is an expanded state, an altered state of consciousness. Reflect on an experience of an orgasm, which starts with physical sensations in the body but moves to a moment of release, a temporary transcendence of the body, an expansion into a non-differentiated bliss state of consciousness. This is soul merging with Source.

Knowing your true identity as a soul, transcendent of physical reality and connected to a larger identity as part of God, Goddess, Spirit, Nature, the Cosmos, can open awareness to the realization that the deepest part of you is more than your body, more than who you think you are. Think about a balloon. When you pick up an empty balloon, all you have is a flat, formless piece of elastic rubber with a small hole in one end. When you blow air into that little hole the balloon fills up into a form. You might say *"it comes alive."*

Let the air out, it loses its shape, its substance, as if it expired with the loss of air. Where did the air in the balloon go? It went back into the surrounding invisible field from which you drew your breath to fill up the balloon. Notice, however, the air when inside the balloon is the same substance as the invisible field of air. There is only a thin membrane of rubber temporarily separating the two substances. Imagine that membrane is the ego identity believing with all its might it is separate from the field with a life of its own. When ego thinks about losing its distinctiveness, it gets very frightened.

Ordinary consciousness is a culturally-conditioned, consensual state in which ego-self appears to be isolated from everything else *"out there."* You experience *"reality"* through the lens of beliefs you have been conditioned into seeing through that your culture defines as *real*.

EXERCISE

Get your journal and review the beliefs listed below Write down your responses to each belief – agree, disagree.

You are your body. You are your ego. You are separate from everyone and everything else.

Life is about competition, survival of the fittest.

There is a winner and a loser in all transactions.

Bigger is better. More is better.

Violence is inevitable toward the 'other' in times of threat.

Humans are better and more important than all other life forms.

Nature is external to us, is to be controlled and used for our benefit.

Time is linear.

The nuclear family is the norm.

If you can't see or measure it, then it doesn't exist.

An expanding consumer-based culture constantly striving to produce more and more goods is the best economic system to improve life for all.

When you have finished journaling allow yourself to notice the impact these beliefs have in your life. Do they enrich your life? Do they constrict it? Notice if you feel an impulse to revisit these beliefs. Remember, beliefs can change.

*****

Not all cultures have these beliefs, nor has our own culture always had them. Yet so long as we hold them as truths, we uphold the cultural lens that doesn't let in any other possibilities. The science of quantum physics that explores reality on the smallest possible levels tells us that we are essentially electromagnetic wave fields of light capable of perceiving a much broader bandwidth of cosmic energies than the beliefs we are locked into by our social conditioning.

Opening to a wider bandwidth of consciousness and opening our belief system for review can transform our understanding of life and of death.

It can help us tap into the creative wisdom to successfully meet the challenges of change that the many world crises are throwing in our faces, our wallets, our health, and the very fabric of life on this planet. Expanding consciousness from the small ego-self identity into identification with a larger sense of self that is unified with the cosmos can also serve to reduce anxiety and fear in facing physical death.

A first step to expand consciousness is beginning to notice how often you are unconsciously reacting to stimuli, like a programmed robot. A wise elder once said the most effective prison is the one you don't even know you are in. If you are *asleep,* i.e., unconscious about your conditioned state, you have no power to change your experience. Noticing brings a *witness function* to your awareness, the ability to observe thinking and behavior patterns that are automatic and reactive, running your life without you even knowing it. Various forms of mindfulness practices can help develop the witness function. Honest feedback about how others see your behavior can be invaluable in waking up as well.

Early in my career at a social service agency treating drug abuse, a respected colleague told me he had observed me being hurtful to others with how I spoke to them. He said I had personal power to get people to do what I wanted them to do but I was doing so in an abusive way.

I was totally shocked because at that time of my life I didn't believe I had any personal power.

Yet when I looked at the incidents he told me about I saw the truth in what he was saying. Indeed, I did have personal power but in not seeing or owning it I was closed off to using it skillfully. My ego defense system had imprisoned me inside walls I did not know were there. Not only did I have to accept the power, I also had to face a shadow side of myself that at times treated others in a disrespectful manner. The honest feedback from a friend was a huge wake-up call to unconscious behavior, which in turn allowed me to start learning how to use my power to influence others in a more skillful and respectful manner.

Another way to help gain release from *the tyranny of culturally based ego consciousness* is exposure to belief systems and cosmologies of other cultures, ancient and current. This opens the viewing lens to different perception about the nature of reality and how the universe actually works. Many ancient cultures used orally-transmitted instructional teachings for those physically dying, as well as for the living, that provided maps of the territories found in altered, non-ordinary states and how to navigate them successfully.

Shamanism, indigenous humanity's oldest spiritual practice, developed many experiential "technologies" that trained initiates in the responsible elicitation and navigation of altered states of trance-consciousness. The emphasis was always practical, returning from the trance with tangible information pertinent to the survival of the tribe, such as where to hunt for game or warning of an impending attack from an enemy tribe.

The trans-cultural shamanic *journey* is the proto-type of the trance state, most often elicited by sensory overload brought on by prolonged, repetitive drumming, fasting, long hours of dance, chant and other brainwave effectors, or by sensory deprivation – immersion in dark caves, arduous vision quests and pilgrimages to sacred sites, and the skillful, socially integrative use of psychoactive materials. All these methods offered an opportunity for experiential exploration of altered states of consciousness.

Forty years of annual weeklong vision quests in the High Sierra while fasting in solitude at extreme altitude after a strenuous backpack into the wilderness melts away boundaries of perceptual separation. Sinking into nature, my awareness begins to feel part of the granite boulder I am leaning against for support. I feel myself in unity with the passing clouds overhead, the pine trees rustling in the breeze, the mountain cliff across the valley, the gurgling creek whose song sings through me. Separation disappears. I am joined in oneness with all that is.

Yet you don't have to fast in the wilderness to have this experience, for ordinary life provides ample opportunity if you are open to it. Witnessing the miracle of childbirth, a beautiful sunset, sexual ecstasy, deep meditation, prayer, getting lost listening to or playing music, long distance running, along with dreams, reverie, contemplation, meaningful religious ceremony and the responsible use of psychoactive substances can all be doorways to altered states of expanded consciousness and identity.

The dynamics of death and dying are central to opening this doorway. To leave the ordinary state of consciousness you have to release the ego's hold on *what is* and surrender into the mystery of the unknown. The old state has to die temporarily in order to gain passage into expanded awareness states in which you can experience a part of you that doesn't die, it just melts back into the larger field, like the air released from the balloon.

Facing death and befriending it as an ally along with learning how to responsibly elicit and skillfully work with naturally occurring expanded states empowers fruitful living and fruitful aging. Doing this work in conjunction with developing the witness function will better prepare you to face what could be challenging waters when the time comes for the final release following your last breath, exiting your body back into the *"field"* from which it came. Perhaps then you will be able to gracefully *"graduate."* As a 14 year-old boy I worked with expressed to me the day before he died, *"We all have assignments in life",* he said. *"When we finish, we graduate."*

A student asked his teacher,
"When should I prepare for my death?"
"Oh", said the wise one, '"you don't have to worry about that until the day before you die."

31

"But I don't know when that will be," replied the student.

"Exactly," said the master.

EXERCISE

Make sure you have your journal with you. Close your eyes. Take some time to induce your relaxation response. Slowly begin to imagine being on your deathbed, your life coming to an end. Notice whatever thoughts, images and feelings arise. Welcome it all without judgment. Just notice the truth of what rises into your awareness.

How do you envision the precise moment of your death?

What are your worst fears about dying?

What do you want your dying to be like?

Are there poems, prayers, music, songs, or sacred texts you would like recited or performed?

Anything you would like to taste, to smell, to touch?

How would you like your surroundings to be decorated and what objects would you like around you?

What state of consciousness would you like to be in when death comes calling? If you want to be peaceful, calm and conscious at the time of your death, then you need to cultivate and practice those states in your daily life starting today. There are no guarantees about tomorrow. If fact, it never gets here, it's always today!

What practices will help you develop those qualities?

Whatever those practices are today is the best time to start working them. Each successive day of your practice you deepen a groove in your brain embedding the new quality and behavior that you want to grow stronger.

Who would you like to be present at your deathbed?

What would you like them to say to you?

Imagine them arriving, your final visitors. This is the last chance for healing and completion of relationships, to forgive and be forgiven, to share love and gratitude, to bring closure to the life you have lived and to say goodbye. *What would you like to say to those who have assembled around your deathbed?*

Take all the time you need to record in your journal your responses to these questions. Then check out Dr. Ira Byock's suggestions to see if you covered the bases for completing relationships as death draws near:

"I am sorry for any pain I have caused you. Please forgive me. I forgive you. Thank you. I love you. Goodbye." (Dying Well. Ira Byock)

*****

You can also befriend death and enrich your

living by composing your will. Start now by picking up your journal and begin recording your thoughts covering the following:

Precise and clear instructions about your dying process. Describe what kind of medical treatment you want at the end, as well as what kind you don't want.

Give clear instructions on how comfortable do you want to be, drugged or not and if so, partially or totally.

Address what you want done with your body and your possessions after your death. Also what you want done in observance of your death. Make sure you tell someone you trust where your will is located and make sure you get the final copy notarized.

*****

Writing up a clear will is a loving gift to your self and to those who come after you so they will not be stressed wondering what you wanted. Don't make others do your work for you. It also serves as a final communication of your values. You can get good guidance in writing a will by obtaining an *Ethical Will Resource Kit* through the Ethical Wills website, http://www.ethicalwill.com. You can obtain the helpful *Five Wishes* through the website www.agingwithdignity.org.

A closing thought from Stanford Research Institute Professor Willis Harmon and former president of The Institute of Noetic Science encapsulates the efficacy of expanding consciousness from ego identity and befriending mortality to enrich living.

"At the level of deep mind we appear not to be separated from one another or from the earth or the universe. Our ultimate sense of security appears to come from full recognition of this oneness."

Chapter Three

Reclaim & Repair:
Finding Your Wisdom Elder &
Healing Your Relationships

*"Aging is an art form complete with its
own separate unique gifts and advantages...
the deteriorating body allowing the mind/soul
to take precedence and grow/manifest and
harvest the seed experiences and
fine tuning of a life-time."*

—James Hillman – *The Force of
Character & The Lasting Life*

Advancing years alone can initiate a significant awakening into the truth of personal mortality, which, in turn, invites reflection on how you have lived your life so far. Entering the older years is an opportunity to reconnect with your soul path, attuning to the deeper urgings of your heart, and focusing creativity and caring on what has the most meaning for you.

Given that many of us spent a lifetime working at jobs to pay the bills and support our families, jobs that didn't give a hoot about our souls or deeper meaning, it is natural to now want to do what feeds the soul through a sense of deeper purpose, values and meaning. Then you can feel good about how you are living and the legacy you will leave behind.

You will, however, have to overcome mainstream western culture's ageist attitude towards older people and the process of growing old itself. Witness the huge market in anti-aging products. In contrast, many indigenous cultures around the world still respect, honor and utilize the wisdom of their elders to help mentor the next generation. Unfortunately, our youth- oriented culture has gone in the opposite direction and older people are too often warehoused, ignored and forgotten.

Some of my fondest memories of time spent with indigenous peoples around the world involve Guadalupe de la Cruz, my adopted Huichol spiritual grandmother whose picture, taken 10 days before she died, graces the cover of this book. She and other elders were treated with respect and appreciation. It warmed my heart to see youngsters, teenagers and young adults making sure the elders were always fed first as we sat around the fire for a ceremonial meal. The elders were looked up to and utilized as teachers, guides, mentors and role models for living a good life and reprimanders when these ways were transgressed.

This respectful way of holding elders that utilizes their potential in socially integrative ways needs revival in the modern world. Mythologist Michael Meade speaks to this potential, inviting us to develop and live out an archetypal, inner wisdom-elder, who carries vital stories in our soul. This potential is both a promise and a challenge. *"Olders"* become *"elders"*, he says, by descending into their depths to find inner meaning, thus freeing them from believing they are *"washed up"* and constricted by fear of approaching death. *"Life is fatal,"* says Meade, *"so get on with the work of finding your gift and bringing it forth."* In his book *Fate and Destiny: The Two Agreements of the Soul* theologian Mathew Fox echoes this call:

"Elders search in their heart for the lessons and experiences that are the foundations of wisdom, bringing their inner soulfulness into community as a voice against injustice, teaching the young that there is a path beyond violence, beyond aggression to creativity, sharing stories that reinforce feelings of connectedness, and 'cosmic citizenship,' creating an inter-generational wisdom where young and old support, challenge and awaken each other."

How the wisdom-elder archetype might manifest for you will be unique to your individuality, perhaps as a Guide, role-modeling new ways of being that honor aging, and the contributions older folks can make to society. Perhaps it might manifest as a Teacher, a Builder, a Guardian, a Spiritual Warrior, a Contemplative, a Wounded Healer transforming suffering. Perhaps as a Playful Trickster, an Explorer, or an Artist. Maggie Kuhn, founder of the Grey Panthers, posits five additional, inter-related roles for older people: as *"Mentors, Monitors, Mediators, Mobilizers, and Motivators."* All of these archetypes live in the inner depths so going deep within in order to nurture their growth is a necessity.

Deepening calls for letting go of control, surrendering, and going to a larger, spiritual sphere that embraces others and their story. These are the same dynamics encountered in befriending mortality.

"In the first half of life," says psychologist David Powell, *"you focus mostly on 'My Story' and 'Our Story', your traditions, family, group, community, country, and your religion."* "In the second half of life you begin to focus on 'The Story', wherein you realize you play a small but vital role in something greater than yourself, a cosmic story found in a sense of interdependence with others, our world, the Earth, our Creator."*

I recognize my small but vital role in something larger than myself in my experience as a grandfather concerned about the future of my three grandsons. I feel a heart-driven urge to share all I can from my experience to support them in facing challenges to come when I am no longer here. This addresses a need many of us share for a sense of continuity that soothes the soul.

EXERCISE

Pick up your journal, place it in your lap and close your eyes. Deep breathe in. Slow breathe out. Take a few moments just watching your breath cycle gently flowing in and out. When ready bring your awareness down to your beating heart. Ask your heart what matters most to its health and happiness. Notice what enters your awareness in response. Ask what matters most to your integrity and need for continuity. You might want to make some notes in your journal so you don't forget what is coming through. Don't worry about any of it making sense. Just write whatever comes into your awareness. Later you can refer back to your notes for reference and support in your journey

*****

Welcome longevity as a gift of evolution, a gift that invites releasing a negatively framed, adaption and coping relationship to aging to a positive one that posits continual growth and development. Accept your longevity as an invitation to find the gifts of your perhaps hard-won wisdom teachings, ones that nurture your capacity to love and to be loved. The aging years are the prime time to live the truth of your wisdom and the wisdom of your truth with, as the Sioux Indians say, *"Oh Mitakuye Oyasin"*, All my relations. In the end doesn't this provide the most meaning in a well-lived life?

A positive attitude about the potentials of aging entails releasing from mainstream cultural messages promoting youth, productivity, material acquisition and striving to *"get ahead."* The path of fruitful aging invites you to slow down, turning attention inward to find and harvest what wisdom you have learned about life. Wisdom doesn't come automatically with advancing years. Wisdom grows as a result of what you put your attention into and the quality of your attention.

I had a recent dream that made me look deeper at what of my own conditioning might need to be released in order to access wisdom. In the dream someone was trying to break into my room and kill me which I frantically tried to stop. Waking up and reflecting on this dream intuitive guidance advised turning the dream around. Instead of defending myself from death, might it serve better to examine if there are any beliefs or ways of being that might actually need to die? Maybe the dream was trying to help me look at a part or aspect of myself that had outlived its usefulness and for something new and good to born the old had to die? When I followed my intuitive guidance I saw that the dream was telling me that what needed to die was any behavior patterns that tried to defend ego.

This kind of inner confrontation aligns with what psychiatrist Allan Chinen calls for in his book *Fairy Tales and the Second Half of Life*. In it he stresses the importance of self-confrontational soul work with empathic understanding of human nature. It calls for *"An examination of attitudes about aging, about limiting beliefs, attachments, and identities, breaking free from social conventions and regaining the spontaneity of the child but uniting it with mature judgment, and turning from youthful preoccupation with things and accumulating possessions. It's about breaking down old routines to make room for new growth, delving into the unconscious to grapple again with psychological issues left over from youth, and facing old fears with the experience of age providing new strength to do so."*

An example of grappling with issues left over from youth involves my early attempt to deal with anxiety and fear through physical strength and toughness. At 13 I started training with weights to build myself up from a skinny asthmatic kid lacking self-esteem, in and fearful of bullying from older, bigger kids. I idolized champion weightlifters I read about in magazines. I wanted to be just like them. So I trained hard, got bigger and eventually became one of the strongest guys in high school. Nobody bothered me. As a result I inculcated the belief that physical force was the way to success in life. When the going gets tough, tighten up, get ready for battle, push, use force to get what I want and be successful.

As an adult I no longer use physical force or the threat of it to get what I want but the pattern stayed hidden in my subconscious. Many times I created stress by pushing when it wasn't the appropriate response to the situation. One time in a meeting I was leading with the staff of a drug program where I was the treatment director I was trying to convince them to try out my idea of adding a wilderness treatment project to supplement the already existing services we were offering our clients. I presented my ideas, answered questions and got positive feedback from everyone. But I didn't stop there. I kept pushing my idea, harder and harder, louder and louder, trying to force my will on the others. I had built up such a fear of rejection in my mind beforehand that I wasn't able to see the staff's acceptance when it was right in front of me! Finally a psychiatrist on the staff stopped me in mid-sentence, *"Tom, you already have our acceptance and support. You are fighting a battle that is already won!"*

Working with children and young adults dealing with the ravages of life-threatening illness I learned about a different kind of strength, an inner one that far surpasses the physical pushing power of big muscles and physical force. Watching the courage, dignity and grace they showed in dealing with painful treatment procedures, surgeries, amputations, bone-marrow transplants, marrow extractions, etc., repeatedly showed me an inner strength that blew my mind. My old beliefs about what constitutes real strength withered away.

Since one aspect of wisdom grows from paying attention to what no longer works and letting it go, while simultaneously paying attention to what does work and doing more of that; this new understanding about what constitutes real strength is vital to fruitful aging.

We are all enrolled in the *learning academy of life*. We all eventually graduate. The only real issue is whether you find and harvest the wisdom-teachings of your life, synthesizing their lessons from past experience to live fruitfully and graduate with honors: feeling good about your time here and what you did with it. This developmental task calls for a skillful review of experience which meditation teacher and author Ram Dass says can *"awaken ourselves to who we are now."*

In my search for process-tools to *"skillfully"* awaken and harvest life-wisdom teachings, I was fortunate to come across the work of Dr. Abe Arkoff of the University of Hawaii. I had met Abe in the early 1980s when my daughter Kimberly was a student in his psychology class. Abe was doing pioneer work in positive aging way back then but I didn't take notice of it at the time because, being in my forties, aging was not on my radar. Now in my sixties aging was definitely making a prominent appearance on my radar and I was delighted to find Abe had created a *Third Age Lifebook*.

The core of the Lifebook is fourteen *reflective questions*. Each question has its own chapter with exercises, discussions, quotes, theory and examples to stimulate response in an engaging manner. I use this workbook as a key component of my Recognition Rites Honoring Elders Program. I encourage you to order a copy of this excellent guidebook. It will be an immeasurable aid in your harvesting process. (Professional Image, 2633 South King St., Honolulu, Hawaii 96826 for $15.07. http://www.illuminatedlife.hawaii.edu/pages/siteindex.htm. Phone: 808-973-6599.)

Drawing from Abe's questions and adding some of my own thoughts I offer the following points of reflection as foci to help you search for and gather up your wisdom teachings. Believe me, you have them. They are in you. It's just a matter of recognizing them for what they are – learning gems about life. Reading the questions over with a sense of curiosity and adventure as to what they might turn up will help you discover lessons learned and the wisdom they carry, sometimes even in situations that when you actually experienced them felt like failures or mistakes.

I suggest reading one question, then closing your eyes and simply watching what memories, thoughts, feelings, images and voices come forth as you examine your life experiences staying watchful as a prospector looking for nuggets of gold. Keep your journal with you so you can take notes capturing on paper what ever feels significant. Don't worry whether it makes sense or not. Keep your critical sensor out of the process and enjoy the exploration.

EXERCISE

Got your writing materials? Good. Let's go. One at a time.

#1. Look back over your life to find crucial turning points, highs and lows, losses and gains, victories and defeats and major challenges. Using the lens of perspective grown over the passing years what do you see these experiences taught you about life?

#2. What helped you get through your most trying times?

#3. Who were your biggest button-pushers and what did they help you learn about or develop?

#4. Who were the key support people in your life; what did they give you? What did you learn from them?

#5. How do you define success in life and what do you think is most important in living a successful life, a good life?

#6. Do you think life has meaning and purpose and if so, what?

#7. What makes you happy?

#8. What are you most grateful for about your life?

#9. What is most important for you about maintaining well being as you age?

#10. What are your plans, hopes and dreams for the final cycle of your life?

#11. What gives you a sense of comfort about getting older?

#12. Is there anything else you would like to learn about, accomplish or do?

#13. Do you believe you have something to offer others that could be useful that is not being shared and if so, what might that be?

#14. How would you sum up in one sentence your wisdom-teachings from life to pass on to the younger generation?

When you have finished reflecting on these questions and recording in your journal what has come forth give your self a pat on the back for doing this important work. You now have raw material to dig deeper into over time drawing forth ever more insight and learning.

REPAIR

Don't be surprised that in doing this kind of exploration it can bring up unfinished relationship work with your self and with others. Be gentle with your self. This is not about judging or faultfinding. In fact it is opportunity to create healing in situations that perhaps have been stuck in your psyche for years. Welcome them as vehicles for opening your heart, mind and body towards greater wellbeing, health and happiness.

Ask yourself – Does the relationship I have with this person or event open or close my heart? Does the story I carry around in my head about it help or hinder me in my life? Am I stuck in it causing more pain and suffering?

As you review these troublesome situations your answers to some of the fifteen reflection questions above might help you to see lessons learned from painful times that in fact serve you today. Perhaps you can let go of the old story and create a new one that honors the fact that wisdom came through the challenging time that today enriches your life.

Ask yourself – "Any people I need to forgive?

Any people I need to ask for forgiveness?

Do I need to forgive myself?"

If there are unhealed relationships still lurking around in your heart and head it can be he helpful to write a letter to those people sharing your side of the experience and asking for their forgiveness and or giving your own. But don't send the letter! Give yourself some time to sit with it for a while and see how it might feel to be on the receiving end of what you wrote. If after the passage of time you feel good about the healing potential in what you wrote, then go ahead and send it (if the person is still alive and you know how to reach them, if not, you can ceremonially burn the letter the smoke carry its message to whom and wherever it needs to go).

It is vitally important however to let go of attachment to a positive response from the recipient. Healing comes from releasing what has been clogging you up with guilt, shame, anger, bitterness, sadness or whatever so your heart and awareness can once again open to the love that lives within. Love is for giving. Forgiveness frees you up so you are no longer holding on and you can go on with your life with more light and ease.

I wrote such a letter to my deceased dad, Fred, in my mid-twenties. In working with a hypnotherapist I discovered, to my shock and shame, a subconscious anger towards him for dying and leaving me. I wrote this letter in response:

Hi Dad.

I'm so sorry you had to die so young. I barely knew you, and then you were gone. The memories I do have are of loving times we shared but I grew up sad and missing you. I wish you could have stayed around longer. I am angry that you left me. I felt sorry for myself and grew bitter in my teenage years.

Now I'm grown up with a loving wife and children of my own. I hope to live a long, healthy and happy life and really be there for them in a way that you weren't. I know you didn't want to die. I am sorry you missed out on seeing my sister and me grow up and now your grandchildren too. I forgive you, Daddy.

Thank you for the love you gave me while you were here. I love you. I still miss you but I carry you in my heart. Losing you at such a young age left a huge wound but it taught me about impermanence. It took a good 20 years but eventually it helped me see and value life because of its fragility and preciousness. It grew me into an adult who appreciates each day and each relationship and into a career that helps others do the same. It was a hard learning path in those early years but with hindsight now I see and appreciate how it enriched my life.

Thank you, Dad. I love you. Your son, Tommy.

*****

It is possible you might need to write a healing letter of forgiveness to yourself, and if so, do it from the perspective of a higher and unconditional loving presence. I urge you to write any letters that you need to in order to free up previously blocked thoughts and feelings so your life force can flow more freely.

When you've finished your letter writing go back to your written responses to the reflection questions. Hunt through them seeking the wisdom of truth and the truth of wisdom. As hard as it may be see if your life-review work offers additional opportunity for honestly facing wounds, failures, grief, shame, guilt, grudges, hurts, resentments, anger, envy, self-pity, victim-hood, bitterness, negative judgments, feelings of unworthiness and anything else in your shadow closet that constricts you with upset and suffering. This may be frightening to consider doing but the rewards are worth it. By facing the truth of what lies within you the door is open to creating conscious relationship with it instead of being victim to it which weakens your life force.

Remember that courage isn't the absence of fear, courage is going ahead with what needs to be done even when your knees are knocking and your heart pounding. Have faith in the possibility of healing. There is immense transformational power within you that can be tapped.

Healing starts with noticing how you hold painful events in your mind. Notice your mental frame of the situation, the story you tell yourself about it. Notice what impacts that frame, that story you carry around in your memory about that person or situation, has on your mood, your body and your energy. Are you contracted around it? Are you a victim? Are you stuck in the past with a closed heart?

While it is not possible to change unfair, unjust and undeserved events from your past, it is possible to change how you hold them in your mind. It starts by acknowledging that it is not the event itself that causes pain and suffering, it is the relationship you have with the event in your mind, i.e. how you think about it and the way you relate to it. I can't change the fact that my dad died when I was very young. But I can and have changed how I relate to this fact from a relationship that initially had me angry and bitter to one that today recognizes how it grew me in many positive ways that enable me to help others dealing with loss in their lives. In truth, you have the ability to change your relationship to the event or person from a disempowering one to an empowering one. Easier said than done but still, it is possible.

When I was a teenager, my unresolved grief about my dad's death brought forth an array of acting-out delinquent behavior, which included shoplifting. I was usually very successful at it. That is until age 15 when a department store detective apprehended me as I tried to leave with several shirts and a bathing suit beneath my jacket and pants. The detective said he knew what I had done and would let me go if I showed him what I had hidden under my clothes. I believed him. I took off my jacket and that instant a policeman entered the room and arrested me. Bitterly fuming at being lied to I promised myself that one day I would find this man and exact revenge.

Over the years my angry promise went underground as new events took precedence. Many years later in a deep state of reflection on vision quest in the High Sierra I realized the bitterness of my anger story of betrayal was still in me contributing to a closed heart. Since I wanted healing, I realized I needed to reframe this whole situation. First, I acknowledged how I hadn't been taking responsibility for this event or others in my life, blaming others for my pain. I had to admit this pattern was still going on. Obviously in retrospect I was in the wrong to shoplift, the store clerk was just doing his job as he saw fit. I saw that for the healing of my heart I had to forgive him and then forgive myself as well. I went down into my heart to sent love to him. I wished him well in his life. I sent love to myself as a hurting, confused and shamed young teenager.

I saw how bad I had felt in seeing the anguish in my parents' faces (my mother had remarried three years after Fred, my biological father, died) when they came to get me from the police station. I saw in reflection how this incident had been a key factor in changing my acting-out behavior because I saw how much pain I had caused for people that I cared so much about. I reframed how I held this event from a poor-me victim story to one I was thankful for because being arrested woke me up to take a more responsible role in shaping the kind of life I wanted to live. In owning my role in what had happened and in sending love to my teenage self, a life-long pattern of blaming others for any difficulty in my life started to lose its power. My heart opened, a subterranean pressure released that I hadn't even known was there.

You too have choice about how you hold painful events from your past in your mind. Denial, distraction, repression, and projection are unskillful energy-draining ways of dealing with pain. Bottom line, if you don't transform your painful relationship with the person or event, you stay in a victim state blaming others for your woe. Change your relationship with the past event by changing your mind, changing your thoughts. Change the wound into a sacred scar.

Unfortunately the mental model that many of us were brought up in is a fear-based, faultfinding one that produces pain and suffering through judgment, guilt and shame. What's needed is a new thought system, a new set of beliefs and behaviors and a new way of using the mind based on the wisdom of love, kindness, and compassion. Love is always present, invisible yes, but still present, just like the air. We just have to learn how to access it.

In this regard I was fortunate to work for thirty-two years with life-threatened people as a clinical consultant at the Center for Attitudinal Healing in Tiburon and Sausalito, California. The Center used attitudinal healing principles and peer support groups to help people find inner peace no matter how disturbing the circumstances. It was an ordeal by fire but I learned a totally different way to use my mind than what I had learned growing up.

Attitudinal healing is a cognitive pathway using the mind to reach the heart. It rests on three premises: First,

There is good within us all given by grace from the creative wisdom intelligence of the universe. Peel away the layers of identity based on physical body, personality, persona, and personal life history. Keep peeling until you get down to the rock-bottom core of who and what you really are at the center of your being. There you'll find your true identity, a luminous energy constellation whose nature is infinite, unconditional love.

The second premise of attitudinal healing: **It is possible to tap into the love energy at the core of your being anytime, anywhere.** How? Intend it. Everything starts with intention. Then take hold of your attention. Shift your focus from head to heart. Connect with your love-essence, it is always there in your heart waiting for you to come calling. Similar to the middle of a cyclone with its always calm and peaceful center amidst destructive winds howling around it, the gift of love at your center is always there. It never really leaves. You leave it by unskillful and unconscious use of your mind. Negative judgments about yourself or someone else, guilt, shame, not being present in the moment and living in the past or the future all close your heart, blocking the awareness to love's presence.

The task is to remove the blocks to your awareness of love's always-present presence. Whatever helps remove the blocks to reconnect with the underlying love is healing. Why let love waste away imprisoned in the constriction of judgment and fear? Your love is needed in the world. You are the only one who can give the love that lives in your heart.

This connects to the third premise of attitudinal healing: **The purpose of love is for giving.** Every moment of being alive is an opportunity to open your heart, extending unconditional love out into the world. Like a gardener watering her garden, hook the hose up to the spigot and turn on the faucet. Like an old song from the Bellamy brothers, *"Let your love flow to all living things."* Not the conditional love of the marketplace, love that says, *"If you do what I want, I will love you. If you don't, I won't!"* No, that won't do. We have enough of that kind of love. Instead send unconditional love given freely without wanting anything back.

Start by giving it to yourself as forgiveness.

Let go of perfectionist expectations. Remember you and everyone else you meet and know is a spiritual being having a human experience in the school of life, a school where everyone is a teacher in one way or another, especially so for those who push our buttons. Button-pushers provide opportunity to face and re-own shadow projections, since what you judge in another, you judge in yourself. Button-pushers expose your shadow, the parts or aspects of yourself you don't like, wish weren't there or wish were different, that you are ashamed of or frightened of, and defended from, all of which cuts you off from your inner light and true nature.

Carl Jung speaks about the individuation process in the second half of life as facing the shadow and bringing its contents into the light of awareness. You grow into wholeness by creating fruitful relationship with those parts of yourself that you previously denied or ran away from. Button pushers help us do this work by triggering our reactivity so we can see the forces at work, and then address them consciously.

How many times have you found you are judging someone for something that under honest scrutiny you know darn well you have done in the past and most likely will do again in the future? An examined life evidences that we are all students and teachers to each other and that in any given moment we are either giving love or asking for it, though the asking may at times be unskillful or even hurtful. Bottom line, what we give to another, we give to ourselves, what we judge in another, we judge in ourselves. Finding and applying the wisdom teachings of our lives and healing our relationships offers immeasurable help as physicality diminishes with passing years for the challenges and loses of aging can be offset by learning how to be more loving to our selves. It all starts with intention.

EXERCISE

Ask yourself:

Right now, this very moment, what do I want to experience —
Love?
Peace?
Happiness?
Feeling joined and connected with others, with life, with the Universe, with spirit?
Or –
 Would I rather experience -
Pain?
Suffering?
Conflict?
Fear?
Feeling separate and alone?

Not to choose consciously is a choice, a weakening one, because it allows the pain-producing conditioned software already imprinted in the unconscious to run the show, producing more suffering.

I don't know about you but I have had enough pain in my life. To the degree I have choice in the matter, I choose opening my awareness to love's presence and inner peace. Working at the Center for Attitudinal Healing for so many years in stressful situations I found that I could have that outcome more often than not if I did three things:

1. **Choose inner peace as the only goal.** For example,
   "I choose to experience inner peace now," not, *"I choose to experience inner peace now, and be right, or win, or be applauded, or liked,"* or whatever your condition may be.

2. **Extend unconditional love and forgiveness to whomever and wherever you want to send it.** Be what the children at the Center called a *"love- giver"* and *"love-finder"*, instead of a *"fault-finder"* and a *"love-seeker"*.

3. **Listen to your intuitive heart guidance.** This doesn't mean to reject the rational mind. Rather it addresses a cultural imbalance in our educational system whose emphasis is based on developing the qualities of rational, logical sequential thinking to the detriment of the intuitive quality, which perceives the whole, not just its pieces or fragments.

EXERCISE

Try an experiment. Think of a button-pusher in your life. Think about what they do that pushes your buttons. Then go inside and notice how you feel, your energy state, and your mind state when this person succeeds in pushing your buttons. Now take a few cleansing breaths to release this energy. Slowly begin breathing down into your heart. Fill it up with light. Expand the love with each in-breath brought down to your heart. When you have that going, bring in your button-pusher. Imagine them standing there before you. Send out a beam of love energy from your heart right into the center of their heart. Not to change them, not to make them be different. Instead, thank them for being in your life as a teacher, one who shows you where you are attached to wanting them to be different and having it your way. Notice any resistance, allow it to be and just stay with the process.

See their behavior that bugs you as an unskillful attempt to get love coming from a frightened insecure place in their being. Fill their hearts up with light. Keep sending them love, gradually visualizing it expanding out of their heart into their body. Let go in trust that they are getting it and being helped by it at some level of their awareness. Make sure not to not seek confirmation of it or expect any recognition or thankfulness from them. Your job is just to give love. If you want something from them then your giving is conditional and that doesn't do the job. Only the unconditional love that gives for the sake of giving does the trick.

Focus all your attention on sending this

love-light into your button-pusher for sixty seconds. Allow your heart to soften, freeing you up to experience a greater sense of ease and wellbeing. Notice what you experience in your body, your energy level and your emotional state as you do this. You may observe a shifting from a contracted place to a more open one where you are no longer victim to the button pushing behavior. If you find yourself unable to do this, accept whatever your experience is in the moment without judgment and simply send love to yourself, honoring where you are. Notice where and how you might be holding tension or tightness. This is an opportunity to be compassionate with your self, to be gentle and tender. Trust where you are. It is not a contest, a competition, or a race or a pressure to be something you are not. Send love and unconditional regard to yourself. You deserve it. Notice any differences in your mental, emotional and physical state from before you began the exercise.

*****

This exercise is about noticing the impact of being more loving to yourself, to others, using your mind to open your heart. It is about the application of wisdom towards repair and life enrichment. Using your mind in this way contributes to what is called the *"hardiness personality."* A person with this trait deals with the pressure and stress of difficult times effectively while retaining their health and wellness. A person without the hardiness factor breaks down. There are three components of the Hardiness Personality, the three C's, and are part and parcel of attitudinal healing.

The **first component** is *Commitment* to a meaningful purpose. **Second** is a *Sense of Inner Control* so that you don't feel victim to external events. **Third,** having a mental outlook that views disturbing situations as a *Challenge*, an opportunity to explore how to be with the situation in ways that you can learn something from it, using it to grow instead of a personal attack. One friend says this is about changing your perspective about the situation from being an *"upset"* to it being a *"set-up."* The set-up perspective says this is an opportunity to choose consciously how you want to respond, reactively or skillfully. This is what psychologists call *the power of the cognitive frame*.

I remember an eight-year-old boy with cancer who was frightened about going to the hospital for his needle drip of chemotherapy. I helped him learn how to induce his relaxation response by traveling in his imagination to a favorite place where he felt safe, comfortable and enjoyed being there because he was having fun. I helped him practice this technique until he became quite fluent with it and able to enter a very peaceful trance state. When he went in to the hospital, we arranged a phone call just before the treatment began where I guided him back into his trance state. He went into the procedure very calm and relaxed.

His mother called me several hours later to tell me how it went. Turns out the little guy did great. The needle went in without problem; he remained in his peaceful state aptly demonstrating his innate ability to access his center of inner peace in a stressful situation. There is one other part to this story however. Seems while he was lying there getting the chemo, a nurse inadvertently bumped into the gurney, which jarred the needle out of his arm, and they had to start the whole process over! His parents were angry, the nurse felt horrible.

What did the little fellow do? He remained peaceful, turned to the nurse and his parents saying, *"That's OK. It was an accident. You didn't mean it."* In that moment the child was being a teacher for the grownups, sending love energy instead of attack, blame or shame energy. He stayed peaceful while the needle was placed into his vein and the infusion continued uninterrupted.

The wisdom of repairing relationships with self and others literally holds life-enhancing power strengthening resilience no matter what age we are but especially in the elder years. Physicians today know the effects of long-term stress, pain, anger, and loneliness cause physical harm to our bodies by weakening the immune system. Hundreds of studies show that skillful use of the mind can enhance immune functions and healthier hearts since thoughts trigger emotions, which trigger release of electro-chemical energies into the blood stream that do one of two things, create ease or create dis-ease; which one depends upon how we use our minds.

In fruitful aging we want to strengthen

resilience on all levels of our being so it is vital to find, own and use the wisdom teachings of our lives using our minds and attitudes to promote health, happiness and inner peace. To illustrate how important these dynamics are consider the role of mind-set in the event of a solar eclipse. For our stone-age ancestors this was a catastrophe. A sky monster was devouring the life-giving sun. *"Will it ever return? Are we doomed?"* Today, the same event brings large crowds out to enjoy it with awe. In the first case the event causes stress. In the second case the same exact event produces excitement and joy. One frame is fear-based, the other is positive. We humans are meaning-making beings and it is the meaning we make of an event that determines our felt experience, not the experience itself. So making meaning of our lives and using our minds with wisdom in a skillful manner for love and loving is key to aging fruitfully.

The good news is that is it never too late to tap your life wisdom teachings using them to create positive optimistic thoughts to enrich the quality of your life. A Harvard Medical School Health letter of 2012 reports on a thirty-year study with hundreds of people documenting how optimism alone links to longevity.

Teddy Owyler, a vibrant, lovely 90 year-old shares her experience harvesting her wisdom teachings for fruitful aging.

Teddy

"I am old now, near the end of my life. Most important for me through these last 50 years has been checking to see if I am ready and ok about dying. To not be afraid, to feel finished or up-to-date with those feelings is comforting for me. One night I found myself thinking, 'Well, maybe this is it, maybe I'm dying' and immediately everything eased. I sank sweetly into the bed and was at peace. I do wish for the energy to be a Hospice volunteer again and to skip rope on Saturday mornings, but I am quite ready to say goodbye and feel my energy shift into the energy of the universe.

"I am content most days. I cherish silence and space. Being in nature fills me up and makes my heart open all the way. I keep learning and *exploring. My challenges are a monkey mind that churns when I don't feel well: What did I eat? Did I forget my meds? Did I do too much? When my ego slides into unskillful control, I am miserable so I stand still and check out my reactions.*

"Sometimes I forget 'no' is a complete sentence and I go fast trying to do too much. I am better now at just letting go when my body is misbehaving. I am pacing myself better, resting when I need to, feeling comfortable about not attending every splendid gathering or celebration or opera or meeting or exercise class.

"Social contact, keeping in touch with my kids and their partners is a part of my life I am most proud of. Gratitude and adoration nourishes me, it fills me up. Seeing friends, phoning, visiting, near and far, is a large part of my life's mural. Though I am alone a lot, I'm never lonely. I read. I sleep. I watch the birds. And I am deeply attentive to Magic Johnson, my precious cat.

"The most important thing I have learned in my whole life is the inner peace of eliminating judgments. That brought harmony into every moment. I have preferences, but there is always wiggle room. I no longer try to change what is".

Nancy Corser, an octogenarian, also speaks to the importance of finding and using the wisdom teachings of one's life.

Nancy

"I have learned that there are many things I have no control over - only my response to them. I just try to keep remembering that. What is most important is to keep my response to aging upbeat and positive——that's what makes it fruitful.

"One of my main challenges was when my husband John died. I was 61 and he had been in my life since I was 15. We grew up together and he was the dominant partner so I had to learn how to do for myself with everything.

"I was determined not to lean on my kids. I refused to be like my mother - whimpering 'poor me'. I joined a spiritual support group that helped me work with my grief in a positive way. I was lucky

to still have a career that I liked (nursing). I also found out that walking really helped anxiety and did fun/walking outings with anyone who would go with me - gotta keep movin! I started a regular activity program—line dancing (you don't need a partner), I joined a gym to help me maintain strength and balance. I took up yoga and I eat a well balanced diet keeping my weight down.

"I also have such fun taking my grandkids on trips—-I get to live vicariously through them. The key for me is continuing to reach out, take chances, smile and laugh often. It's so important to stay active and engaged and positive!"

*****

Teddy and Nancy are wonderful exemplars of fruitful aging, putting the wisdom teachings of their lives into daily practice. If you do not have a blood family to relate to as Nancy does with hers, you can create supportive relationships with others who share your values and interests. There are also volunteer opportunities in children's organizations that hunger for elders who have tapped their life wisdom-teachings to be supporters and mentors for their kids.

Remember that wisdom is different than information and knowledge. The Internet today provides unlimited information and knowledge regarding anything you wish to learn about. But wisdom is more than knowledge. Knowledge informs. It is possessed. Wisdom understands knowledge, it transforms. Real wisdom is living what you know. It emerges from quality attention paid to what matters most in life – how it works. Longevity is the gift of time to learn from your life experience, and then to apply it.

The Japanese have a valuable wisdom tradition called *Wabi-sabi*. It is an attitudinal and perceptional training to pay attention to what is important. It holds a positive valuation about older people, older things and aging itself by finding beauty in nature, accepting the natural cycle of growth, decay, imperfection and death, while revering authenticity above all.

Wabi-sabi finds aging objects interesting, fascinating and beautiful as they transform over the years. It embraces liver spots, rust, and the march of time they represent. It reminds us that we are all transient guests on this earth, our bodies along with the material world around us all in the process of returning to where we began.

Sabi by itself means *"the bloom of time"*, a kind of beauty that can come only with age, the lines in a person's face that let us know how much they have laughed, loved, cried and dealt with adversity in their lives. *Wabi-sabi* offers a refreshing perspective on aging that supports the harvesting process of finding the wisdom teachings of your life in order to live fruitfully the remaining years of your life.

May your wisdom teachings transform challenges into opportunities for enriched living and loving. May you stay open to surprising opportunities that may present them selves that call for something you have learned that will support others in ways you couldn't even imagine. The following story illustrates this point in a very dramatic situation but know that what you know can be helpful to someone everyday just in the course of ordinary living.

Long ago in Japan, high on a mountain by the sea there lived an old farmer named Hamaguchi. With him lived his grandson, Tada, who called him Oji-san, which means grandfather in Japanese. Tada loved his grandfather dearly and revered him for he knew he was old and very wise.

At the base of the mountain, near the beach that skirted a bay, was a village. Many of the villagers fished, but the food that was their mainstay was the rice they grew in their fields on the mountain beside the long, winding road that lead up to the rice field of Oji-san. Their rice fields were precious to the villagers. In spring they planted each precious rice seed, and in summer tended each precious plant. In autumn, when the rice stalks turned golden and dried in the sun, they were stacked, ready for the harvest that meant food for the entire year.

One day in autumn Oji-san and Tada stood on the balcony of their house looking out over the golden rice fields down to the village. The crops had been good this year and there was going to be a celebration in the courtyard of the temple. People were stringing colorful paper lanterns on the houses and putting banners around the temple.

The air was still and heavy. Oji-san noticed the banners were not moving.

"It feels like earthquake weather," said Oji-san. No sooner had he said it than the house started to rock. It wasn't a strong enough quake to frighten Oji-san, he had been through many earthquakes. But this one was strange...a long, slow shaking as if caused by changes far out in the deep sea. As the quaking stopped, Oji-san's keen eyes looked out to the sea. The water darkened suddenly...it was drawing back from the beach... the sea was running away from the land! Oji-san and Tada saw the villagers running from the streets and from their houses, all gathering on the beach. The water kept drawing back, baring the sand. There were fish jumping on the wet sand, delighting the children, but the people were perplexed, they didn't understand...but Oji-san did. He remembered stories of long ago told in his childhood and he understood what the sea was going to do. He had to warn the villagers! But how could he get a message down the long winding road... there was no time to tell the priest to sound the bell! He had to act. "Quick!" he said to Tada, "Light me a torch!"

Tada lit a torch and gave it to his grandfather. The old man took it and ran to the field where his dry rice stalks stood, ready for harvest.... his precious rice...all of his work for the last year, all of the food for the year to come. He thrust the torch into the dry stacks and set the rice on fire... they burst into flame; sparks flew up into the air.

Tada ran after his grandfather. "Grandfather, why? What are you doing?" he shouted. Oji-san didn't have time to answer...he had no time to explain...he was thinking only of saving those by the edge of the sea.

Tada ran crying into the house. He was frightened. He thought his grandfather had lost his mind. Oji-san went on, setting fire to stack after stack of dry rice stalks until his entire field was afire.

Down below, the priest in the temple looked up and saw the blaze on the mountain. He set the big bell booming. When they heard it, people turned from the beach and began running up the winding road to put out the fire. The young men were the fastest; then came the mothers and fathers with their children and the old people too...all running to help put out the fire. Oji-san watched... "Faster, run faster." he whispered.

The young men arrived first and started trying to put out the fires. But it was too late to save the field of Oji-san. They stood and stared at him in sorrow. Then Tada came running from the house. "Grandfather has lost his mind," he yelled. "He has gone mad! He set fire to the rice on purpose!"

"You set the fire on purpose?" some of the men shouted angrily. "The old man must be mad," others murmured. "Next he'll set fire to our fields!" They looked at him threateningly.

The old man raised his hand, pointing toward the sea. "Look!"

The people turned to look. There at the edge

of the horizon, they saw a long dark line of shore where no shore had been before...it was moving toward them...that long line of darkness was the returning sea... towering like a cliff, yawning like the open mouth of a monster... coming toward them more swiftly than dragon kites.

"A tidal wave!" The shout went up. Suddenly, all the shrieks and all the shouts were cut off by the shock of the great wave striking the shore with a force that sent a shudder through the mountain. There was a burst of white foam like a flash of lighting, and spray that went up the mountainside. When they looked again, they saw a wild, white sea raging over the place where their homes had been. It drew back roaring, sucking, tearing out everything as it pulled back...and then it struck again...and again and yet again, though each time with less strength. Finally, the sea returned to its place...leaving only wreckage behind.

Around the house of Oji-san, there was a shocked silence. No one spoke. There was no more village, only scattered pieces of thatch along the shore. Then, quietly, the people knelt and thanked Oji-san for saving their lives".

Chapter Four

Revitalize Your Heart Path With Vision & Purpose

*"He who has a why to live can bear
with almost any how."*
—Basic Writings of Nietzsche

The Huichol Indians of Mexico believe that every living being has a path of heart to walk on to what they call *"completion"* at the end of their lives. They go on an arduous pilgrimage through mountains and deserts to awaken their *"iyari,"* their heart memory, to *"find their lives"* and the power by which to live it. Indigenous peoples throughout the world believe we are not here in this life by accident. They believe the Great Spirit breathed life into us and gave each of us special gifts (*"medicine"*) with a purpose in being here – find those gifts, develop them and share them for the greatest good, growing into the fullness of who and what you are.

I found this to be true in my own life when

my love of music led to a startling experience with a hospitalized child. I play a little guitar and love to sing even though I can be off-key and my musical skills are rudimentary. Nevertheless, when a youngster from the Center for Attitudinal Healing asked me to come visit her in the hospital and bring my guitar, I was nervous but didn't want to let her down.

I walked into the hospital room she was sharing with six other kids, one in a semi-coma state in a crib. She filled me in on how things were going, then, *"Hey Tom, sing me a song!"* Feeling self-conscious and inhibited, I nevertheless picked up my guitar, strummed a few notes, and then started singing. I sang a folk song we'd sung together a few weeks back at the Center. Jennifer and I were singing along when suddenly the three-year-old in a semi-coma opened her eyes, stood up in her crib and started to dance. Nurses rushed in. Squeals of delight filled the room. I was stunned, totally amazed at how music could produce such a dramatic outcome. It is a perfect example of how you don't have to be a whiz or great talent, just follow your heart and go for it. You never know what can happen.

Many indigenous peoples around the world engage in various types of vision quest rites of passage fasting in solitude in the wilderness. This is done initially at the time of adolescence helping the young person to find their gifts and a vision of their life purpose. It also helps them create a relationship to a power greater than themselves to help them live out their vision. Entering the elder years also calls for a vision quest of sorts; one seeking deeper guidance on how to best live out whatever remaining time you have to renew, revitalize and fulfill your purpose.

Dr. James Hollis, author of *Finding Meaning in the Second Half of Life*, provides context for such a quest:

"During the second half of life you are called to serve something bigger than yourself; you have to have an eye on being all you can be for yourself, those you love around you and the planet. You have to try to be in the moment and give to the people around you as much love and knowledge as you have to share."

Hollis advises beginning your quest asking – *"As an agent for the highest good, what would be fruitful for me to know or do? What are the undernourished aspects of my soul that cry out for attention? What talents, interests, fantasies and dreams want to be nurtured and expressed before my life is over?"*

Seeking deeper vision at this later stage of life doesn't necessarily involve going out into the physical wilderness, though it might, ass Ron Pevney's wilderness work with elders (listed in Helping Resources at the end of this book) amply shows. What a quest for purpose and meaning in the elder years does call for is the adventure of exploration in one's inner wilderness bringing the light of conscious awareness into the fertile dark of the unconscious. The turn inward is for deeper listening – to reverie, to reflection, to intuitional attunement that allows the voice of what Jungians call the Senex or Crone, the inner masculine and feminine wisdom-elder to be heard. Ask questions — *What is the meaning of my life? What higher values am I here to serve? Am I living so I will be remembered for what I want to be remembered? What needs healing? What wants expression? What aspects of the psyche are out of balance? Too much masculine? Too much feminine? Too much intellect? Too much feeling? Not enough?*

It's a quest to find who you are now and how you can grow into greater harmonious attunement with the essence of your being. In youth it was about the search for identity. Now it's about shifting identity from a separate ego self towards a perception of the deeper part of your being that is connected to nature, humanity, the cosmos, the universe Power is sought as in youthful quests, but not for control over others or for physical strength, but instead for inner strength, standing up for the truth of who you are, and what has greatest meaning for you. Ironically, the deepest inner strength comes from surrendering to a power larger than you.

The older quester braves the inner wilderness facing the inherent mystery, paradox, ambiguity and uncertainties of life. Mystery is not something to figure out intellectually. It is something to pay attention to and learn from in order to live with its challenges towards greatest maturation and fulfillment. Carl Jung notes, *"All the greatest and most important problems of life are fundamentally insolvable ... they can never be solved but only outgrown ... some higher or wider interest appeared on the person's horizon, and through this broadening of their outlook the unsolvable lost its urgency. It was not solved logically in its own terms but faded when confronted with a new and stronger life urge."*

You can nurture the life-urge towards full blossoming by seeking the truth and purpose inherent in your deeper being. Respect, receptivity and trust in surrendering to the wisdom of inner knowing are key qualities in freeing the creative life force within that wants its chance to achieve its fullest potential while there is still time and energy to do so. As a friend once mentioned — *Surrender and come over to the winning side.* Coming over to the winning side entails acting on inner guidance to live from the luminousity of our deepest being and supporting others in doing so as well.

Recently I sat with a friend doing some deep soul-work. We looked at the difference between giving up and surrendering. Giving up is quitting, often accompanied by feelings of failure, frustration, despair, anger, resentment, bitterness, self-pity, shame and blame. Surrendering, as explained to me by my first Native American teacher, is about consciously taking your load of troubles over to the altar of spirit and releasing it over to the divine power of the universe. This exercise works what I call *the faith muscle.*

Faith is about releasing and letting go of trying to control everything. It is about trusting the greater process by letting go of fear, worry and doubt. It is about opening heart and mind allowing sacred mystery to bring through wisdom guidance on how best to respond effectively to address the problematic situations that arise. It is not about passivity. It's also not about responding with unskillful reactivity coming from fear. It is about opening to non-egoic wisdom guidance about how to respond in a manner to bring through greatest good for all. As a friend of mine says, *"Remember to Surrender. Surrender to Remember."*

Gratitude is key in this process because a thankful heart brings harmony, what the Navajo call *"hozhoni."* Gratitude requires awareness in recognizing the blessings in your life. It promotes happiness and wellbeing. It is a causal force raising your vibration rate, which cosmic consciousness responds to by sending more to be thankful for. It is no surprise that the happiest people are the most grateful people. They live in purpose, they live on purpose, and their lives are rich with meaning.

One can even have gratitude for challenge. This doesn't mean excusing or allowing abusive, hurtful or unjust behavior. It means holding challenges in a wider context that recognizes them as potential vehicles to grow in some significant manner for the betterment of your own life and the life of others. The mystical tradition of Kabbalah offers an interesting perspective on this with its concept of *"Tikkun Olam,"* healing the world.

Drawing on a cosmological vision received in the sixteenth century by the Rabbi Isaac Luria, it sets human purpose as raising consciousness by doing good in the world, or as Luria calls it, *"raising the sparks."*

Here is Luria's vision that came out of a seven-year solitary sojourn on an island in the Nile River. See how it resonates with your own seeking of deeper vision of purpose and meaning.

At the beginning of time, God's presence filled the universe. When God decided to bring this world into being, to make room for creation, God first drew in a breath, contracting. From that contraction darkness was created. And when God said, 'Let there be light' (Gen. 1:3), the light that came into being filled the darkness, and ten holy vessels came forth, each filled with primordial light. God sent forth those ten vessels, each carrying its cargo of light.

But the vessels were too fragile to contain such a powerful, divine light. They broke open, split asunder, and all the holy sparks were scattered like sand, like seeds. Those sparks fell everywhere. Each particle in the physical universe, every being, every thing, is a shell that contains sparks of holiness. Our task is to release each spark from the shell and raise it up through acts of loving kindness, being in harmony with the universe and through the medium of higher awareness.

That is why we were created — to gather and raise up the holy sparks, no matter where they *are hidden. When enough holy sparks have been gathered, the broken vessels will be restored, and Tikkun Olam, the Repair of the World, will be complete. It is the task of us all to raise these sparks from wherever they are imprisoned and to elevate them to holiness. In each moment of existence we have the potential to raise holy sparks. If we are unaware of this ability, we are spiritually asleep and miss the boundless opportunities because everything in daily existence presents sparks locked in husks awaiting release. (*Kabbalah of Creation: The Mysticism of Isaac Luria: Modern Kabbalah)

While this vision is hundreds of years old its call for releasing the sparks from their husks is still timely today in relationship to revitalizing your heart path with vision and purpose. What call do you hear when you listen in to the voice of your heart and soul? What lives in your dreams, your hopes, and your vision for this last cycle of your life, for life itself, for the world? What happens when you revisit the passion of your youth, your earlier spiritual strivings, the passion that was perhaps squashed or put on hold while raising a family and making a living?

Conscious aging specialists George and Sedena Cappannelli urge that we *"Experiment with new attitudes and new practices. Take risks; let go of what does not work and what is familiar and comfortable for the sake of new discoveries, new opportunities and new horizons. Listen more closely and carefully to the wisdom that comes to you from your soul and act in accordance with it. Seek to live a life of greater balance in which collaboration, cooperation, inter-dependence and, above all, love for your fellow beings, are your guiding principles."* ("Do Not Go Quietly", Peregreen Books)

EXERCISE

Here is a creative imagination exercise for helpful clues towards revitalizing your sense of heart-path purpose. Imagine you have unlimited funds to start a foundation. What kind of work would your foundation be doing? See it successfully happening. What would the rewards be like for you, for those helped by what your foundation offers? How do you feel experiencing the successful fruition of your foundation's purpose? See if you can write up a mission statement for your foundation. Give it a name. What measurable goals and timeline might you create? Play with this and see where it takes you. Have fun.

******

Here is what happened for Phil Sheridan, a seventy-eight-year-old retired librarian who honored his soul's love of story. Today, he shares stories with young children in library readings and also with fellow retirees in senior citizen homes. He takes great joy in handpicking his stories and *"in people enjoying me as I do the sharing."*

Phil is comfortable with his mortality. As he says, *"It is a given."* He doesn't fret about it. He believes in something higher and thinks life would be joyless and grim without it. Phil says it is only in the last ten years that he found meaningful purpose for his life. The major wisdom teaching of his life, realized in retirement, is to not be afraid of giving or receiving love. He notes this is easier said than done but he is working on it diligently.

Phil Sheridan

He hopes to be remembered for a legacy of love and kindness. His advice to his aging peers is passionate and clear – *"Read stories regularly to four-year-olds!"*

Phil's life took a turn for the better when he journeyed into himself to see what wasn't working and to start exploring new ways of being that did work. He searched for and identified the wisdom teachings of his life, found his vision and purpose and gets revitalized each time he goes out to share stories.

Like a snake shedding its old skin with faith and trust that something new and good is coming dare to venture forth to live out your deepest vision and sense of purpose as Phil did. It can be a great help to remember that you are not going forth alone. In fact, don't even try to do it alone. The creative power of the universe is with you and wants to act through you. Philosopher Martin Heidegger's puts it this way; *"A person is neither a thing nor a process but an opening or a clearing through which the Absolute can manifest."*

How about opening up and inviting the *"absolute"* to manifest in you? You can get its power for free every day coming up from the growth power in the Earth, from the light of the sun in the day and stars and moon at night. You can also draw on the power of the four cardinal directions as indigenous peoples around the world do for each direction has a different gift. Face each one and see if you can find what it offers you.

There is also power at your own center connecting you to all that has been, is now, and will be. The *"absolute"* is always present, closer than your next breath. It gave you your life with its heart-path purpose, it maintains your life with protection, it gave you the gifts within and it gives you the power and wisdom guidance to live to fullest fulfillment and completion.

Sometimes exercising your trust muscle and surrendering into the Absolute can be pretty scary but that what it takes to fully realize your vision and heart path. Here is a real life story to support your process of doing precisely that. It takes place on another white-water raft trip on the Tuolumne River several years after my first terrifying one. The river was running at a considerably lower rate than previously so I hoped for a less stressful time and more fun. The river had other ideas.

Once again the raft went over Clavey's Falls and lo and behold, I was knocked out of the boat into the mouth of the foaming abyss. There was one significant difference this time however. Prior to setting out our river guide explained that if anyone fell in at this spot and was sucked under we shouldn't resist the downward pull. *"Don't fight against it. Don't give up. Don't quit. Just let go."* He explained there is a downstream current at the very bottom of the hole. *"If you get sucked down, just go with it and you'll hit the bottom stream, which will push you out into the downstream current. You will be all right."* Wow, talk about surrendering with faith and trust!

As I went overboard I remembered the river guide's counsel. I surrendered. I let go, hoping dearly that as I plunged down into the depths he knew what he was talking about. It was a literal experience of releasing into bigger power than I certainly had. Plunging towards the bottom of the washing machine like-vortex I thought to myself, *"Man, I hope that sucker is right about this!"* In an instant that felt like eternity I hit the bottom current. It immediately shot me out of the hole back into the main current flowing downstream. I stroked madly to the surface and gasping for breath made it safely to shore. Hallelujah! I was alive!

It certainly wasn't by any heroic effort of physical strength on my part. Instead, doing the opposite from my instinctual response to fight hard was what saved me. It was about surrendering and letting go totally releasing with faith and trust into larger power, a manifestation of the *"absolute"*.

Thank goodness for the river guide passing along the wisdom of memory from past experience, what Native American story teller and poet Joseph Bruchac calls *"the long memory"*. Memory shared saving a life.

Long memory, heart memory, lives in you and connects you to your purpose in being here. May your vision quest to your inner wilderness help you find your heart-path purpose and create a revitalized relationship with the Absolute that enables you to age consciously and fruitfully.

> *Think back before the word titanium*
> *think back before the word uranium*
> *the word missile, the word obsolete.*
> *Think back before talking machines*
> *think back before recording machines*

think back before machines
who think like men
you will find the long memory there
it is walking around
sharing a story with trickster
it is drawing within moist sand
placing the palm in dye
made of bark
pressing it flat against
dry stone.
Place your hand there
it may fit the lines
of your life.
Now listen
to keep the long memory
is the hardest
most dangerous
thing we can do.
Yet it is all that
saves this world
for our children.
Now listen
now remember
this poem
of long memory
which will never
forget you.

—*Our Stories Remember.* Joseph
Bruchac

Chapter Five

Reawaken the Power of Creativity, Courage & Generativity

"Courage is not the absence of fear, but rather the judgment that something else is more important than fear."

—Ambrose Redmoon, *Gnosis: A Journal of the Western Inner Traditions*

When I was a young boy I worked really hard trying to comprehend infinity. I'd gaze up for hours at the stars at night wondering, *"OK, if you got on a space ship and went to the end of the universe, well just the fact that it ended meant there had to be something on the other side!"* I just couldn't get it; my mental fuse box would short circuit.

It wasn't until a visionary experience in my early twenties that I was gifted by grace to have an experience in which I finally not only intuitively understood infinity, but also solved another quandary from childhood – *"What does it mean that we are created in God's image?"* Since I had rejected at a young age the notion of deity as a stern, old, white man with a long beard sitting on a throne in the sky judging us, I had no clue what to make of this conundrum.

The vision took place during the same LSD experience in which I saw the existence of unconditional love as the basic reality of creation. In the altered state of transformational journey I saw in a vision my whole ancestral line going back to the beginning of time. I saw the impact of their experiences shaping their minds, values and belief systems and how that was both passed on to succeeding generations and shaped further by their experiences leading all the way up to me.

I saw how my entire notion of what is real, who I am, and what life is about functioned as an outer covering of cultural and historical conditioning, which up to that moment I'd thought was all there was to me. But the vision showed that underneath the external shell is infinite creative energy, which is how we humans are made in the *shape* of our creator, *"God's image."* It isn't about an external form at all!

At our essence, under the shell of belief about who we are, what is possible and what is real, is this infinite creative energy in which the only real limitations to what is possible are the ones that we create in our minds. I saw that if we open our minds and show up courageously with one hundred percent effort on our parts, then and only then, do we find out what is possible. To create steam from boiling water you can't stop at 211 degrees - you only get hot water. One more degree and you get steam that can take a hundred-ton locomotive over a mountain!

If we show up and give our best shot and it doesn't work out, then we need to let it go, trusting that it wasn't for the greatest good but at least we went for it and tried. The vision also showed that full-hearted effort, i.e., generativity, going for whatever is the *"it"* of your life, opens new doors that hadn't even been imagined before, especially if the work is done with an open heart and without attachment to the outcome. Focused yes, desiring yes, but not attached and holding on out of fear or desperation.

I recently took my family to a baseball game where our local minor league team was playing a visiting team from Hawaii. The night was special because Bill Lee, a former major league all-star pitcher for the Boston Red Sox, was on the mound for the local team. He had flown out for this special occasion, a one-night stand you might say, trying to be the oldest person to ever pitch and win a professional baseball game. Bill was 65 years old.

The stadium was full of older sports fans like myself, people who remembered Bill from his major league days, as well as younger fans and families who came to see what happened at this celebrity event for a small town. Bill was always a character who spoofed seriousness and pretension but he came out to the pitcher's mound that night with a determined look on his face.

I was nervous for him. He had a big protruding belly that hung over his pants. He walked with a pronounced limp. *"Man, poor Bill is going to get lit up by these younger dudes. It's going to be embarrassing for him. These guys are all young athletes in the prime of their fitness, their reflexes and strength at their finest. I bet Bill doesn't last through the first inning!"*

Bill warmed up taking it easy but when the first opposing batter came to the plate Bill threw a fastball that showed he still could bring it. The man had some heat left! Each batter he faced hit the ball solidly but, fortunately, it was directly at a fielder so three up and three down. Bill made it out of the first inning. I felt relieved. He hadn't been an immediate failure.

When it was Bill's turn to bat he faced a tall, lanky fast-baller who threw major heat. *"No way Bill is going to be able to swing that bat fast enough to hit this guy's pitches,"* I thought to myself. Wrong again. Bill hit the ball every time he batted, including a run-producing single later in the game.

As the game wore on, Bill stayed with it though he was losing speed on his fastball. Fortunately, he had a variety of other *"junk"* pitches that proved difficult for batters on the Hawaiian team. True, he wasn't as fast or strong or quick as the younger players but he was crafty. He was smart. He used his experience as an elder to play wisely. Both pitchers didn't allow a hit until the middle of the game. The visitors got four runs off of Bill but the locals came back and got eight runs of their own and held the lead going into the fifth inning. *"I bet Bill is going to let a relief pitcher come in now so he can rest up. He'll get the credited win if the other team doesn't score more than three more runs. He's gotta call it a night now."*

I was on a roll of wrongs! Bill continued to pitch that inning and every one afterwards. He pitched the whole game, nine innings! He won! The oldest man ever to win a professional baseball game! When the last out was recorded, ,Bill doffed his hat to a roaring crowd. He bent down to the ground and kissed it. Standing up again he met a throng of baseball fans, who had stormed the field to get his autograph. What an amazing night, what an amazing feat to see this guy old enough to qualify for Medicare compete successfully against guys who were three times younger than him!

Driving home that night a voice kept running in my mind – *"You just really never know what is possible unless you show up and give it your best shot. Then you'll find out. You doubted the possibility of Bill's success and look what he did. His mind was open. Open your own mind and go full-tilt for whatever calls you. And by the way, don't forget to have a good time while you are at it!"*

Bill's threshold for fruitful living was the baseball field. May you find and step over your own unique threshold into fruitful aging that contributes your creativity and wisdom gifts to the world. What you have to offer is needed but you have to show up and do your work to bring it through. Don't let the inner or outer nay-sayers hold sway. Walk up to the metaphorical pitcher's mound, rear back and let 'er go!

I invite you to bolster your courage and take ownership of your wisdom lessons and your heart-felt desires. Access your creativity and generative potential to explore meaningful ways of manifesting your gifts in the world. One place to start: recognize the importance of not allowing what you have learned to disappear when you leave this planet. It will enrich your life to find a way to pass on to the next generation what you have learned. This in itself can serve as a significant purpose guiding your actions.

Opportunities abound to make this happen: inter-generational storytelling, writing an autobiography, compiling a family history, creating artistic expressions of your deeper values via drawing, painting, sculpting, song, chant, creating a play, making a collage, writing a short story, poetry, theatre, however your creativity guides you to express itself.

Other means of creative expression and generativity include mentoring, volunteering, leadership, spontaneous acts of loving kindness, service to others, working with causes that promote peace, social, economic, racial and sexual justice, causes that work to address environmental challenges, that promote non-violence, that offer sustainable ways to live which create win-win scenarios for all life on this planet.

Rest assured, you are not here by accident nor have you lived as long as you have by accident. There is greater purpose in your being here at this time. You have something of value to contribute, to share, and to pass on, something that benefits others. Don't let it die on the vine for lack of courage. Remember that courage doesn't mean you don't have fear or anxiety. It means going forward despite your fear and anxiety, doing what your soul calls you to do.

I had to call up courage a few years ago when, out of the blue while driving down the road, I reached out to turn on the radio and listen to some music. A soft inner voice said, *"No, take your hand away from the radio button. Be quiet. Just listen!"* Words began to flow into my mind as phrases of a song. I started to sing them out loud. *"Wow, I like that! I better pull over to the side of the road and write it down or I won't remember it."* I wrote the phrases down in a journal, and when I got home, I picked up my guitar and fiddled around with some chords. Now I know nothing about song writing, composition or music theory, nor am I gifted with a great voice or musical talent. I just love singing and playing music. Words for new songs kept coming over the next few months. I loved it. I wrote them all down. I could just sit down and think about an idea and song lyrics would come. Like writing a poem, I'd work out the rough spots, find chords that expressed the tune, and lo and behold, I ended up writing fifteen songs.

The need for courage came in when an inner

prompting pushed me further: *"Start singing your songs to other people. They are not just for you!"* Gripped by self-consciousness about singing around others, inhibition and fear about not having a good voice and the clumsiness of my guitar playing, the last thing I wanted to do was to sing out loud in public. The inner prompting pushed harder like a pressure that needs to be released so finally I bolstered my courage and shyly began to share the songs with family and friends.

"Not bad, I like it," some said. This gave me courage to keep going. I started to learn about music theory, song composition and structure. I practiced my guitar and singing. I refined the songs with help from musician friends. Then came more inner prompting and pressure to make a CD of the songs I'd written. Talk about pushing the envelope!

Huge judgment and fear reared their ugly heads. *"Who do you think you are? You have no talent. You are going to make a fool of yourself in public. You don't have the money to pay a producer. Nobody will want to listen to what you do. Don't even try. Don't be an idiot. You are just a narcissistic egomaniac who wants attention. Get a life. Just let this one go."*

Whew. I found that I couldn't argue with these judgments and fears but it helped immeasurably when I also heard an inner guidance voice that encouraged me to keep going. It said that the songs carried an uplifting message and like memes (seed thoughts) my job was to just get them out in the world. What happened after that was not my concern.

I decided not to let my fear, anxiety and misgivings stop me from doing what my heart and soul were calling me to do. I decided to go for it. It helped to remind myself that it was not about having people like it or trying to be a star, making money, or any external rewards. It was about honoring the call of creativity without attachment to outcome or how others responded to it. Instead enjoy the creative process itself. Enjoy the ride, have fun with it.

I am happy to say the CD, *Jumping into the Real – Songs for the Soul*, with a picture of my three grandsons and I in Hawaii jumping off a wall into the ocean, is completed and out in the world. To my surprise, some people are actually enjoying it! Who would have ever believed it? I share below a few reviews from friends not to toot my own horn but because it shows that even when you are not particularly talented you can still bring through creative expression from your soul that can make a positive difference to others.

"I have to hand it to you — the musical arrangement is exceedingly catchy! There's a great mix of Rock-a-billy, Native American, some good old Western style and the harmonica and guitar are wonderful. I loved the odes to your grandsons and the one to your mother. That brought tears to my eyes. You're a true model in putting your heart out there as far as it's asking to go."

****

"I loved your CD. I put it on, on my way into the city and I was laughing and singing with all my windows rolled down and got lots of laughs and smiles from the people who heard it and saw me grooving. Thanks."

****

"Just finished listening to the CD a second time; even better than the first! Definitely puts a smile on my face! "My Favorites:
Wiping the Tears
Sacred Reciprocity
Thank you Plant People
Being a Grandpa
I Am a Sacred Worthy Human Being.
Thank you."

****

"We are driving down the highway 5 and I wanted to tell you how much we're enjoyed listening to your CD as we speed down the road. Powerful,inspiring and beautiful lyrics sounding out from all the songs. Thank you for this gift!"

****

Your own unique expression of creativity awaits your attention and nurturance. Creative potential is there, always has been there. Access to it begins with intention. Take some time to follow your breath inside and just relax for a few minutes.

Give thanks for the presence of creativity within you, even if you don't feel it in the moment. Give thanks to whatever you believe is the source of creativity. Tell that source your intention, such as —

"Thank you for this precious gift. I seek to open to your flow. I will make a good home for it and honor what you give me. Thank you."

You never know what can happen unless you go for it, like Bill Lee. Like me who was kicked out of chorus class in high school because my voice was so bad.

Good news about creativity and generativity for all us aging folks comes from brain-imaging studies about creativity which reveal that while we use both sides of our brain up until midlife, we predominantly use one hemisphere more than the other for any given task. But starting in midlife, people begin using the left and right sides of the brain in a more synchronized and equal manner. Behavioral studies with magnetic resonance images found other qualities that get better with age: amygdales, the portion of the brain that governs emotion are less reactive to fear, while prefrontal cortices, which handle planning and judgment, become more active and there is more control over emotions.

These brain/mind changes point to a maturing of cognitive capacity and performance in midlife and beyond that occur because of aging, not despite it. This enhanced interplay of the right and left-brain appears to be a positive factor for creative expression in the second half of life.

Developmental midlife brain change is also accompanied by the maturing of other key psychosocial domains — emotional intelligence, social intelligence, judgment and consciousness. It seems older adults remain calmer and have greater emotional stability with less attachment to outcome or people's responses, giving them more psychological freedom.

Through a thirty-five year study of psychological development in the second half of life with more than 3,000 research and clinical subjects, Dr. Gene Cohen found that thought evolves in a new way in which we see and understand what we look at and experience in life. He calls it *"post-formal thought,"* where a new synthesis presents a new pathway for creative expression. It's about an inner voice that says to you, *"If not now, when? If not you, who? Why not? What can they do to you?"* Basic message — *"Do not live an unlived life!"* (The Creative Age: *Awakening the Human Potential in the Second Half of Life*, and, The Mature Mind: *The Positive Power of the Aging Brain*.)

Cohen says this inner feeling of liberation bolsters courage to try something new. He points out that the predominance of folk art in the second half of life is an example par excellence of late blooming, noting that it is likely an important reflection of the convergence of brain and psychological development. It seems that elder artists are the rule, not the exception. Many artists do not come to the forefront until after age 65.

Witness a 1980 exhibition at the Corcoran Museum of Art in Washington, D.C., that featured 20 of the best folk artists whose work spanned the half-century between 1930 and 1980. Of these 20 artists, 80 percent were 65 years of age or older when they did either their initial or best work. Thirty percent were 80 years of age or older when they first seriously got involved in folk art.

Cohen refers to the maturing enhanced integration and synergy of cognition, emotional intelligence, social intelligence and judgment as *"developmental intelligence,"* reflecting the maturing of the mind with aging that shows itself as wisdom.

Pulitzer Prize-winning novelist Ellen Glasgow describes her experience of maturing mind — *"In the past few years, I have made a thrilling discovery ... that until one is over 60, one can never really learn the secret of living. One can then begin to live, not simply with the intense part of oneself, but with one's entire being."* (*The Creative Spirit: A Path to Wisdom.* Andrea Sherman and Marsha Weiner)

Gary Topper, a retired 72 year-old businessman talks about his experience accessing creativity and generativity:

"Aging for me has to do with both my mind and body actions. I do everything I can to stay healthy physically and emotionally. The idea of not giving up on life, knowing that there is much

more ahead of me and the idea of giving back, all contribute to the process of aging consciously.

The most important aspects for me are relationship(s), spirituality, and a vital active life that stimulates my mind. Relationships include first my husband, without whom I would not have the drive I have for living the way I do. Sharing our lives, being proud and supportive of each other's accomplishments and the mere sharing the space of life is incredible. Community engagement in activities that support each other's life and the giving back to others with an appreciation for what I have in my life is critical as well.

And finally, activities that keep my mind alert expand my consciousness and ability to age fruitfully. In my case this is learning to speak Spanish, teaching English to Latino people, playing the Native American flute, travel, working with environmental causes and my spiritual community.

I remain extremely active and do as much 'giving back' as I can both because as an elder, that's my work, but also because it gives me emotional and physical life. When teaching English to the immigrant community I'm always in the knowledge that what I'm doing is helping not only these folks but also their families.

Working with social justice and environmental issues not only keeps me in touch with the world community but also with an incredible diverse group of people. Through involvement with spiritual communities and my own spiritual work,

I do my best to ground myself in the present and live life fully so that the wish that I have - 'to die feeling filled up with life' helps me cross over in a good way."

Increasing research affirms Gary's experience, pointing to the importance of meaningful connection with others and indicating how social networks not only shape our lives but also have major impact on our health, wealth and happiness.

Gary Topper

Gary continues....

"Being in a healthy, loving relationship, doing the work of giving back and volunteering, travel and education are the major ways I keep my mind active and hence my body alive. I've come to understand that this is individual work, that is, I have the choice to do none of the above or all of it, and I can see that 'letting go' of life can

be a choice as well. What's very helpful to me is realizing how important it is to move in the world with a 'young-person-attitude', which allows inclusion in anything I want to be involved in. I'm passionate about taking responsibility for my life and making the necessary moves that allow for a rich existence.

"I realize that relationship and community are key factors in creating the strength to move forward. I couldn't have done what I have without the help of my partnership and community, but there is certainly something inherent in my being that doesn't allow me to give up. I also have huge gratitude for what I have achieved and what I have, and with this I clearly understand that sharing what I can becomes the payoff for what I have received."

"Right now I look at the rest of my life as a 25-year period and hope that I can live as much of this period as possible continuing doing what I'm doing now, in a healthy, positive way. I want to fill up the 'tank' so that when I go, I will be satisfied with the life that I have lived. I think about getting to a place that is complete and lets go easily. I struggled my whole life around what spirituality really is, and I'm hoping that what I've learned will be helpful. We'll have to wait and see. I do know and feel good about what I have accomplished and what I do to help others. Other than continuing to enhance my relationships, my understanding of life, doing 'my work' and living a fruitful life, I do not dwell on the end."

Gary's life exemplifies courage to live out his values and his vision of what has meaning and significance. I find it important to remind myself that courage is not the absence of fear or anxiety. Courage is going ahead when your heart calls you to do something even though your knees are knocking, your heart pounding and a part of you wants to run away and hide. Don't shut down your dream by giving all your power to your fears. Grow your faith instead and live the life you were intended to live.

One of the most courageous, creative and generative examples of this is my friend Janie Rezner, a 79 year old multi-media artist, sculptress, musician, composer, writer and social activist with her own radio show. Janie speaks passionately about the wisdom of the *"Grandmothers"* for healing the ills of the earth in her book *A Wake Up Call from Mother Earth.*

"In 1976 I was 43 years old, living in Davenport, Iowa where I had raised my three children. My youngest child had left for college and I was recently divorced from my second husband. I remember thinking that my life was over! Little did I know that on some very deep level, it was just the beginning.

"My homesteader phase was coming to an end. Ahead of me was a time of intense learning where I could more fully expand into new experience without the worries and constraints of youth and young adulthood, yet carrying with me my previous rich life experience as homesteader

and mother to draw upon. I was beginning a new phase of life, drawing inward to the reality of sacred being-ness, discovering great vistas and expansion of heart that lie within me. I was beginning my spiritual quest. I believe we are all being called into the search for Divine. Of course I didn't know any of those things when my journey began.

Janie Rezner

"As we age, and if we have been paying attention, we move with some maturity and life experience, into recognizing that this is the stage of life in which we can become an elder, a wise one, who can reap wisdom from a longer view of life. Aging does not mean getting ready to sit back in your rocking chair and let someone else

do it. You are the elder, the wise one. It rests upon your shoulders to turn this world around — to speak truth — to dare to protect life. I feel that elder women are the ones to speak up, the ones to be listened too. Life has been very out-of-kilter without the wise and cautioning words of the Mother and the Grandmother. We must now step up and dare to be heard. It is the most noble endeavor we can engage in . . . protecting our precious life on earth.

"My profound spiritual journey in aging has opened up vistas far beyond my expectations and often beyond my understanding. My story, my music and art and writing have been an unfolding in ways that I couldn't have begun to predict, imagine or create."

None of Janie's creative expression and generativity would have transpired without the courage to go forward following her heart and spirit-call to develop and share her gifts. Janie believes six ideas are vital towards fruitful aging:

Understand that you are here for a very special reason. Meditate and trust the process you find yourself in. Trust your own feelings and intuition.

Dare to speak the truth.

Stand upon the ground of who you are.

Get serious. Mother Earth and all her creatures need your help.

Do not let yourself be taken off course.

Realize that we truly are the ones called on to make a difference.

Mike Lerner, a retired dentist, found his way to make a difference through creative expression and community service. Here is his story of fruitful aging.

Mike

"What it means to graciously and ferociously enter my 70's is difficult to even language. To live this long is a gift people my age are quite thankful for and usually want more time here. I want to name my own journey. Why name it too small or too vague? I call it the Arc of the Rainbow.

"I had a normal childhood, Boy Scout, good grades, not great but good enough to get into UCLA, then I went to a highly accredited dental school. Got married, divorced, remarried, divorced, remarried over the next span of 45 years or so, 3 children. I prided myself on my role as a successful and skillful dentist, well respected, and as a father.

"I bonded with my disabled son in my care as a single father and with my daughters as close friends, I created a life that was rich in a spiritual community, I learned to play guitar and sing with accomplished musicians, I enjoyed a variety of

friendships with creative, intelligent and conscious people, I played a central role in the evolution of a Men's group.

" Finally, I married a fine woman, Ellen, who appreciated what we could do together as a team and harnessed her wagon to mine so that we could build a home, travel, and share our lives with our families and community around us as we moved into retirement. That opened a new chapter for me unlike any other I had stumbled upon in life.

"Financially secure, healthy in mind and body, I was free to pretty much do what I wanted at the age of 64, 6 years ago. I started to explore the territory of my soul; meaning for me, what it is that I do that aligns with who I am at my deepest level.

"I began to examine what has given me the most meaning, and then decided which of these kinds of actions to manifest into my future, given that the narrowing currency of time has replaced all others as the measure of how I would now pace my life. What am I prepared to do with the time I have left that will yield to me the deep knowledge that I am living my life, bringing my soul out in its most beautiful way? It is only I who can choose that and make it happen. It seems that the more courage I can manifest to choose wisely, to care little what others think, the more creative and fulfilling will be my choices.

"Last June, at the time of my 70th birthday, I finished an art project, the history of my family. From boxes of photographs, recordings and

*written memories of my parents, uncles and aunts,
I wove together the history of our family over
150 years, something my grandchildren will have
forever - how we came to America, our early life
here, and what we were like as a clan. It gave me
a deep soul satisfaction and I dedicated it to my
ancestors. I want to be remembered for following
through on that inner guidance to create that
book, finish it, and for the beauty with which it
was done.*

*"Recently I was asked to help a Rabbi perform
and lead sacred music for the High Holiday
Services for the small congregation of which I am
a member. I worked with the Rabbi and one other
person for three months in preparation. I learned
many new songs and we delivered them beautifully.
Tackling this assignment, and pulling it off was
very satisfying. It required learning strange new
music, and embraced my love for bringing song
and joy to others. I loved the challenge of it all,
including risking being seen nakedly as myself in
front of others.*

*Sometimes I sing with my son in local parks
on Saturday morning. My daughters all play
instruments and occasionally, when we're all
together, we create a little band. Singing and
playing with musician-friends creates exquisite
moments where we become aligned emotionally as
we enjoy the sounds, rhythms and images created
by the words and music.*

*"Sometimes I ponder that had I been blessed
with talent, I might never have really appreciated*

that music in the world needn't be spectacular to be valuable. When I craft and work diligently to learn a song, then play it around others, I know that something deeply connected to my soul is emerging. My humanness, frailty, determination, love of poetry, rhythm, my love for my friends comes pouring out and when I get really lucky, I can see that this love connects us to each other in this moment, and we are singing prayers rejoicing in life, all of life, all of existence. When that happens it becomes unbearably beautiful.

"Daily I am profoundly conscious of the temporality of life, the precarious edge upon which our lives are balanced, and I am grateful for each moment of every day and the gifts that have blessed my life. I try and bring my joy for living into every encounter that I have.

"I visualize my life as a rainbow, arcing across the span of my life, and I am at the right side of that rainbow, closer to the earth, heading back towards the ground, the soil from which I was created."

****

In each of the elder accounts in this chapter there is a repeated theme: every person puts their spirit into bravely following their heart path. As the following Hindu story, *The First Marionette* from ancient India illustrates, this is not a new theme but an old one that brings renewed vitality to aging people.

Lord Shiva and Lady Parvati were walking

through the bazaar when they saw two carved dolls lying on a carpenter's table, their wooden limbs jointed and pegged. 'Let us put our spirits into those dolls,' said Lord Shiva. They did, and the two began to dance.

Soon, a crowd gathered. 'Why they look almost alive' an old woman gasped. Children laughed and clapped their hands. When Lord Shiva and Lady Parvati withdrew their spirits, the dolls slumped to the ground. 'Oh, don't stop!' the disappointed people cried.

Lord Shiva said, 'Carpenter, see if you can make them move.' The carpenter tied pieces of string to each of the dolls' jointed limbs. When he lifted these strings, the dolls slowly rose, at first moving awkwardly, then, as he gently pulled on the strings, they began to dance.

Lord Shiva smiled. 'When you put your spirit into them, you too can bring them to life".
(Spellbinders Collection of Stories.)

Chapter Six

Recognize Your Highest Potential: Growing Spiritual Maturity & Intelligence

"Teach us to number our days, that we may get us a heart of wisdom".
—Psalm 90:12, Old Testament

Fruitful aging results from befriending the challenges of change. It takes intention and skillful means to create a positive, healthy and growth-full relationship with increasing physical and mobility limitations, aches and pain, loss of family and friends, diminishing physical abilities and skills from youth, loss of job-defined identity and a clearly structured role in life to name just a few of the challenges that can come with aging. As Bette Davis famously said, *"Aging ain't for sissies!"* Most of us have seen older people responding to the challenges of aging with rigid, fear-based, repetitive behaviors that shut down vitality and joy.

In contrast, fruitful aging grows out of an attitudinal and behavioral shift from an emphasis on ego identity drives to soul drives and soul-based identity. It's about *soul-nurturing work* remembering forgotten ideals, seeing what can be, not just what is and the reclamation of wonder, delight and imagination in finding magic in the ordinary. It also entails activation of what I call the *"surrender muscle,"* especially regarding the acceptance of loss and facing debilitating health issues.

All my life I have loved running. I regularly won prize money at neighborhood Fourth of July races as a boy. I was a sprinter in school. I only lost one race. In middle age I did long distance running including two marathon races. I loved feeling the wind in my face. Sometimes I felt like a galloping stallion, I'd whoop with joy in sheer exultation. I also loved rock climbing, wherever I could find a challenging wall, be it on a building in the city or a thousand foot High Sierra mountain peak in Yosemite.

But my severe back injury and painful knees in my early 60s said no more – *"Keep this up and you will suffer!"* At first this was hard to face. I didn't like the message. I grieved my loss. I got depressed. I felt sorry for myself. I resented no longer being able to do what brought me so much pleasure along with running in my younger years, like windsurfing, snowboarding.

After allowing time to grieve my loss I surrendered to the reality that the time of those activities in my life was now over. But I reminded myself that this loss could also open up new possibilities that might bring me equal enjoyment. I decided to look at what I still could do.

Well, I can still walk and hike so let me get on with that. There are plenty of steep hills and even a small mountain all in close proximity with tons of good trails. I can mountain bike too. That doesn't hurt because there is no impact from pounding or awkward straining positions that happen in climbing.

I soon found that the slower pace of walking enabled me to notice and enjoy more of what was going on around me than when I previously sped by on a run. I could stop and linger over an interesting spider web, the intricacies of a blossom, and the patterns in a rock that caught my eye. I found that I enjoyed the slower pace and a sharper awareness of the gifts of nature happening all around me.

Bike riding had less of an impact on my body and allowed me to keep up cardio-vascular and respiratory conditioning. I loved coasting down big hills. The wind was back again though there was a lot less hair for it to blow through!

Through surrender and opening to new possibilities I was able to replace loss with a new gain. I think this is how the universe works if only we work with it via our attitude and our intention – seeking to find the new with an open mind and positive outlook. Opening to and exploring new possibilities of relationship to the universe is about spirituality whether we think of it in those terms or not.

From the first time I read T. S. Elliott's, *"We shall never cease from exploration and the end of our exploration we shall reach the place from which we started and know it for the first time"* I was spurred further towards the kind of exploration that could lead to growing spiritual intelligence and maturity.

Both in my personal work and in my work with others I see that a spiritual belief system can be a great ally in letting go and opening to the new. Why? Because beliefs about something more and bigger than your self provides a larger framework than ego with which to hold change. A spiritual belief system gives credence to a cosmic presence throughout creation. It stimulates the expansion of awareness into a sense of connection, unity and relationship with a deeper truth of who we truly are, what we are and the interconnectedness of all existence.

The Dalai Lama emphasizes the significance of this awareness when he states — *"The most important thing for us to know right now is the truth of our Oneness."*

Spiritual maturity represents the highest realm of this kind of self-realization. Ironically, this realization calls for transcendence of the ego self into a transpersonal self fortified in knowing its essential oneness with nature, the cosmos, and the ultimate reality underlying and source of what we see and experience with our senses.

The realization of spiritual maturity is characterized by an open and loving heart, a peaceful soul and *beginner's mind delight* in the here and now. It seeks to love with kindness, patience, and compassion, embracing mystery with flexibility and humility. It views experience in a fluid way, a process that is not fixed. It unlocks creative power by embracing life without conditions both for others or ourselves.

A spiritual belief system in conjunction with a spiritual practice offers resource in meeting the challenges of aging, using them consciously for growth and enriched living. Without it the challenges can overwhelm, leading to despair. I witnessed this personally with my mother Ruth, an amazing and accomplished woman who died at the age of 96.

My mother, a gregarious personality all her life, an avid reader, social activist, neighborhood organizer, classical piano player, and world-traveler, had lost vision in one eye and could barely see out of her remaining one in the last few years of her life. Her hearing was poor, her hands bent with painful arthritis, her short-term memory severely compromised. This, along with the regular news of long-time friends dying brought bouts of depression.

She lived in an assisted living home near my two sisters by her own choice. She was surrounded by caring people and numerous activities but still often felt lonely, isolated and disconnected. She struggled with pain from a recent hip replacement, shuffling laboriously with the aid of a four-pronged walker, which along with progressive heart congestion made simple movement a major undertaking.

Her body increasingly failed her, her intellect grew cloudier, which along with her severely limited mobility, left her more and more dependent on others in meeting her simplest needs. Hardest of all, she could no longer contribute to life in her usual ways, giving and serving. Simple existence became an exhausting grind.

She was a gamer though, a survivor. She faced her challenges with fortitude, grace and determination. Towards the end I flew from California to New Hampshire to be with her for our final goodbye, wondering how it would go. I remembered our most recent phone conversation. Her voice was weak and faltering.

"How did this happen, Tommy? How did I get so old? I still feel 18 inside! But I am ready to go. I wake up each morning disappointed, wondering why I am still here."

My mother died as she had lived, in peace, with family surrounding her as she went through her final release. I sat bedside with her near the end. Most of the time she had her eyes closed in seeming sleep. Breathing was arduous, even with the help of an oxygen tube feed into her nose. I held her hand. I told her how much I loved and appreciated her, how much she had touched and shaped me in my life in ways that were so meaningful and important to me. How lucky I felt to have had her as my mother.

Towards the end she opened her eyes, looked straight into mine and with an amazing force given her weakened condition shared her last words with me – *"Love is the glue that holds us all together."* That was it. She died peacefully shortly thereafter.

Ruth Pinkson

My mother had wisdom from an early age. It was shaped by the force of her personality and having to deal with economic and health challenges as a child along with growing up in the Great Depression. She determined at an early age that she would work for world peace all her life. She'd lost her younger brother in World War II and knew the pain of loss again when her husband, my dad Fred, died at the age of 36, leaving her penniless with a four-year- old (me) and a one-year-old (my sister Ilsa). As she faced and worked through these and other formidable challenges her aging years grew her into a wisdom elder who truly lived a life of love, compassion, generosity, creativity, caring, courage and service to others and nature.

None of this protected her however, from depression, at times deepening into despair in her last few years. My mother was an atheist, and thus was not able to avail herself of the benefits of a spiritual belief system to help her cope with her suffering and loss. A spiritually based belief that there is more to us than our bodies, more to us than our egos, and that the essence of who and what we are is more than the physical, that we are part of something greater than ourselves, makes it easier to find meaningful passage in navigating the challenging waters of loss, sadness and grief.

Over the course of a fifty-year career in the helping professions I repeatedly witnessed how the presence of a spiritual belief system makes it easier to shift mental and emotional states from despair and depression into positive ones.

Martha, 85, is a one example. I met Martha when she was a participant in a support group at the Center for Attitudinal Healing in Sausalito, California where I served as a clinical consultant. The center used the non-denominational, spiritually-based principles of attitudinal healing discussed earlier to help group members learn how to use their minds in ways that promoted a sense of inner peace and well being. Martha was a regular participant until her declining health required that she enter an assisted living home in Northern California.

Several strokes later she moved quite slowly with the aid of a walker, considerably limited in her ability to continue what had been a vital and active life. What Martha had, however, was a belief that she was more than her deteriorating physical body.

She believed that her essence was spirit, that love lived at the core of her being, and that her task was to send love to others. Lying in bed unable to move at times, she thought about friends and family and sends them love.

Martha believed that when she died, she'd be reunited with her husband and others who passed on before her. She didn't fear death. She befriended it. She reviewed her life to discover unhealed places or relationships. She worked hard in therapy and on her own to forgive herself and others, to complete unfinished business and through reflection, drew on the wisdom lessons from her life in meeting her considerable challenges.

Martha continued exploring her creative interests and exercising her mind through painting and her love of music. She kept up social involvement with family and friends through phone calls and email. She bolstered her spirituality with meditation, prayer, reading and listening to spiritually oriented books and CD's.

Martha consciously used the challenges of loss, physical and mental decline and limitation to grow spiritually deepening her faith and belief that even though she was bedridden she was still a vital part of life and living with something of value to contribute to others – her love. She worked to maintain a positive attitude and outlook bolstered by her belief that she was part of something that transcended this life.

Martha created a relationship with her aging that made it a vehicle of exploration right up to the end. She worked diligently to be present and aware in the moment seeking to make the most of whatever time she had left. She used an attitudinal healing question she had learned in her support group at the center, often saying it out loud while affirming — *"Right now is all I have. Do I want to experience it in pain and suffering, or do I want to experience it by opening to love?"*

Asking that question helped get Martha out of stuck mental and emotional states. Maturation of her spiritual intelligence had brought her to the conclusion that her reason for being born and living was to remember that underneath body and personality she was love. She got to a similar place as my mother in recognizing the importance of love but her spiritual beliefs and practices helped her navigate the aging journey with more ease and peace of mind.

It was work with Martha and others like her

that helped me identify the five-challenge-task framework for fruitful aging that constitutes the framework of this book.

Revisioning death as an ally empowering life.

Reclaiming your wisdom teachings and healing your relationships.

Realizing your heart path with vision and purpose.

Reawakening your power of creativity, courage and generativity.

Recognizing your highest potential by growing your spiritual maturity and intelligence.

Each task involves learning how to work with change, how to let go of the old, and how to open to new possibilities, new capacities, new identities and new ways of being. Interwoven throughout is balancing loss with a commensurate measure of gain through deepening spiritual insight, understanding and practice.

Let us remember however that growing older physically doesn't automatically guarantee the growth of spiritual maturity, just as every fruit tree which has the potential to mature into one that provides food, shelter, fuel and beauty to other living beings doesn't necessarily reach that level of development.

It is true that impending mortality can

accelerate a search for a personal relationship with how you conceive of a *higher power*, but it doesn't in itself insure heightened spiritual development. What it can do is activate inward movement seeking deeper meaning and deeper understanding.

Social scientist Lars Tormstam refers to this movement inward as *gero-transcendence.* He identifies it as *"a pattern of the aging psyche characterized by a redefinition of the self and of relationships to others, a new interest in fundamental existential questions with increased spiritual reflection and contemplation shifting attention from doing-mode to being-mode."*

Tormstam sees gero-transcendence as a final stage of life, beyond Eric Erikson's last stage of generativity, an elder's drive to guide the next generation. He believes gero-transcendence is a natural progression towards maturation that *"ties the development of wisdom to an increasingly transcendent attitude toward oneself, toward relationships with others, and toward worldly aims, taking more delight in one's inner world, less fearful of death, increased perceptions of life meaning and integrity, service, generativity and feeling a greater connection to the entire universe."*

It seems that when the natural drive towards gero-transcendence is supported and nurtured, one becomes less self-occupied and less interested in superfluous social interaction. There is a redefinition of time, space, life and death and an increased affinity with past generations. Frequently, there is a greater need for solitude and communion with nature, the cosmos and the spirit of the universe, whatever that is for you.

While the drive is natural, it needs the right nutriment to realize its fullest potentials. It requires a contemplative attitude and commitment of time in solitude to work with issues of meaning and purpose, seeking greater attunement with the sacred. It might even necessitate a new form of exercise, perhaps *"inner-cise"* is a more apt term, one that strengthens the *faith muscle*.

See where you are with your gero-transcendence drive by asking your self these questions:

What do I really believe, trust and have faith in?

Do I think of myself as spiritual or religious?

Has a belief in the divine been present in my life and if so, how and when?

To what degree are my spiritual beliefs important in my life?

Do I have a practices of activating what I believe in?

Do I allow myself to be guided by my spiritual beliefs?

Do they help me deal with fear, stress, anxiety and daily life challenges?

Are my spiritual beliefs active in my healing and well being?

Do I believe my spirituality will help me as I age?

***** *

Working with these questions I recently was reminded about what I trust and have faith in when doing T'ai Chi on the deck in my back yard. Moving slowly I rejoiced in noticing vibrant oak, bay, madrone and ripening fruit trees, blossoming flowers with radiant yellow, blue, white, red, and orange petals, tomato and chard plants growing taller in the garden, all shining brightly in the warm spring sun. I marveled how this abundance of new life comes forth every year, birthing out of what had appeared so barren in the dark cold of winter. New life! So exciting, so miraculous. This is what I have faith in: the great, giving, creative intelligence power of the cosmic cycles of the seasons that continuously brings forth life and renewal from death of the old over and over and over again through the eons of time.

I believe in, trust, and have faith in the wisdom and continuity of the seasons. I believe and have faith in the invisible growth power that miraculously energizes the life that I see each spring in the glories of nature born anew. The Huichol Indians call this invisible power Great-Grandmother Growth" – *'Takutsi Nakaway*. They say she pours forth her growth power into us as well as the plants and trees but that we have to be receptive and aware of her gifts in order to work fruitfully with what she sends.

I deepen my spirituality by welcoming and

celebrating the arrival of Great-Grandmother Growth's abundance each spring. This gives me a larger vista to hold the drama of daily life than my ego's perspective and reactivity. It supports my trust and faith in the invisible presence that produces the physical. It supports me in trying to live in harmony with nature and my own integral nature as compared to living from socially conditioned *shoulds*, guilt, or ego drives for recognition. This attunement with the cycles of the seasons seems to grow my spirituality and nurture the gero-transcendent drive of which Torstam postulates.

Personality psychologist Gordon Allport's work differentiating of spirituality from religiosity can be useful here noting that it is possible to be religious without being spiritual. It is equally possible to be spiritual without being religious. Allport's research shows that a person can go to a place of worship on a regular basis and take part in its rituals but still not experience a felt connection with spirit or even believe in a deity. This is called *extrinsic religiosity*. This provides benefits of social connection and a sense of belonging to a community of likeminded others, but it does not protect from end-of-life distress.

Intrinsic religiosity on the other hand entails a felt experience of connection with a transcendent presence that isn't necessarily connected with any particular religion. You can have this experience without being religious in the sense of going to a place of worship or doing religious practices, without even believing in spirit or God necessarily, just connecting with a higher and larger presence than your ego self.

Allport's work shows an extrinsically oriented person seeks out religion because it provides comfort and security. In contrast, an intrinsically orientated person is motivated more by faith and a search for meaning and purpose in life. Evidence suggests differences in one's religious/spiritual problem-solving style can affect one's ability to cope with adversity. Those with an intrinsic orientation appear to cope better with stressful life events because this orientation leads them to seek meaning in whatever events occur.

Allport distinguishes four styles of spirituality or religiosity:

A self-directing style — Individuals with this style are calling the shots. Though they may believe in a higher power, they rely on themselves to solve/handle any problems.

A deferring style — Individuals with this style are more passive. They wait for God to handle the situation.

A collaborative style — Individuals with this style see themselves as working with God to deal with the problem at hand.

A surrendering style — Individuals make a conscious decision to relinquish those aspects of the situation that are truly beyond their control.

The collaborative style seems to be adaptive in a wide range of situations since individuals tend to feel empowered (with God on their side) and motivated to do what they can to improve the situation. The self-directing style is also generally effective, largely because people tend to fare better when they perceive a situation as controllable.

A noteworthy exception is when the situation is extreme and (by objective standards) largely uncontrollable. In these situations, like the death of a family member, the surrendering and deferring styles are often the most adaptive. When nothing can be done to prevent or undo the event, surrendering control provides an overwhelmed person with relief.

Allport's work supports the significance of growing a spirituality that is active and engaged in daily life for it appears to be a key determiner in the quality of well being in the aging years. It points to the importance of nurturing the gero-transcendent drive towards maturation of spiritual maturity and intelligence elevating from ordinary consciousness where objects appear solid and separate to a consciousness that believes and trusts all creation is intermeshed in an invisible web of connectivity.

The indigenous Hawaiians have a word *mohala*, which means to flourish or blossom. May we grow our spirituality towards its highest *mohala* treating each other and life itself as

Meister Eckhart, a 13th century mystic reminds us – *"It is not about doing holy things. It is about making what you do holy."*

Chapter Seven

What's Your Story?

"What can be more important than to understand various aspects of human mind and learning how to encourage those that are constructive and change those that are destructive?"

—Dr. Tom Roberts

To grow spirituality in daily life calls for a practice, a regular behavioral pattern of loosening ego identity and connecting with the divine. Psychiatrist Roger Walsh offers guidance in developing this kind of practice with his discernment of heart and mind principles that constitute what he calls *"authentic spirituality."*

First, he says, live ethically following the Golden Rule. Unethical behavior that is hurtful to others stems from and strengthens fear, greed, anger, and jealousy. Seeking to enhance the well being of others inhibits these destructive motives and emotions. Ethical living matures through stages. First, it's a practice, then a necessity, finally a joy, says Walsh, recognizing that because of the underlying reality of life's interconnectivity, what you do to another, you do to yourself.

Second, Walsh calls for reducing the incidence and impact of reactive emotions such as fear, anger, greed, jealousy and hostility. Instead, seek to cultivate and enhance positive ones of love, compassion, patience and joy, developing equanimity and what Walsh calls *"affect tolerance."*

Third, shift from a culturally conditioned. consumer-based emphasis on acquiring material objects to spiritually based goals of creating more awareness to honor the sacred in daily life.

Each of these behaviors starts with intention and a willingness to work at them. Concentration training to strengthen the ability to stay focused is vital in the process because if you can't sustain attention on what you want, you can't make it stronger. Consider the words of the ancient Chinese sage Chuang-Tzu —

"When water is still it is like a mirror. If water thus derives lucidity from stillness, how much more the faculties of mind?"

Any kind of mindfulness exercise, such as simply watching your breath come in and out for ten minutes a day, repeating silently *"now in"* and *"now out"* will help build up your *mind muscle*, which is instrumental in actualizing your potentials for fruitful aging.

Finally, Walsh emphasizes cultivating wisdom since it often leads to a generous and altruistic life of service. This is important because generosity strengthens love, happiness and self-esteem and altruistic people tend to be happier since taking time to make others happy makes us happier than just pursuing personal pleasure. It is also true that as people age they increasingly find it is the legacy of their contributions to the world and future generations that gives meaning and satisfaction to their lives.

Walsh's ideas started to make more sense as I entered my sixties. Thinning hair turning white, deepening facial lines and wrinkles, diminishing physical strength, energy and endurance, along with increasing incidence of aches and pains left no doubt that my body and my time were starting to run down. Wisely using whatever time I had left became a major factor in choosing where to focus my energy and attention. I wanted to live mindfully and leave a legacy I could be proud of. I wanted to enjoy myself in the process.

With this in mind I started a group on conscious aging to explore mutual concerns, ideas and experiences about skillfully growing older with other people. Exactly one week later my devastating back injury literally laid me low. But low is where I needed to go to begin a direct experiential exploration of what kind of challenges aging can bring.

Because of the wisdom teachings that came through my injury I now recognize any ache or pain as a signal about something I need to pay attention to. I enter into dialogue with it, seeking guidance about its message and what is needed for healing. This helps me understand how to best move, walk, sit, bend, and pick up objects and what is okay for me to do and what is not.

This perspective constitutes a major attitudinal shift about aches and pain from seeing them as negative to seeing them as something helpful. They help me slow down. They heighten my enjoyment *of the gifts of the ordinar:* like being able to walk, to see, to hear, to feel, to taste, to touch. It heightens an attitude of gratitude, embracing the gift of longevity as an opportunity to nurture relationship to sacred presence. It brings me deeper into the opportunity to age fruitfully.

The impactful significance of attitude is dramatically affirmed in the observations of psychiatrist Victor Frankl surviving interment in a WWII Nazi concentration camp. There he discovered the amazing human capacity to find meaning and purpose in the worst of conditions. Even under these horrible circumstances he observed the freedom to choose his attitude about the experience was still available.

As Frankl points out while you cannot control everything that happens in life you do have the ability to choose how to respond to the conditions and events life serves up. By letting go of what you can't control, you free up attention to what is in your power to control — your thoughts, attitudes, reactions and how you frame the situation. This leads to the realization that the deepest suffering is not caused by events but by the meaning you give the events, how you hold them in your mind, your attitude about them, the story you tell yourself about them that determines what you experience inside.

The transformational impact of my back-healing mantra, *"Infinite light and love is what I see, it is but a reflection of the light and love in me"* convincingly showed me the power of relationship to higher power-presence as a major source of support, encouragement and strength to keep going under trying conditions. It also evidenced how helpful it is in charting a course through challenging waters to have some kind of understanding – a story, a myth (like the visit of a totem helper – the hawk in my case), a fairy tale, a guiding dream or vision that offers illumination along the way.

Author, activist and workshop leader Joanna Macy offers such a story. Macy says we are living in the time of the *"Great Turning."* She calls on aging people to take advantage of our opportunity to *"live the most meaningful lives in the history of our species in which each is called to maximize our gifts so that we can bring about a spiritually fulfilling, environmentally sustainable, and socially just human presence on the planet."*

Macy's story continues. *"Western civilization is going through a rite of passage from adolescence towards adulthood and like all rites of passage there is no guarantee of a successful outcome."*

Macy believes this time and situation we are living in now calls for wisdom elders to help guide this passage into a *"new age of living in harmony and balance with nature in which decisions are based on how the effects will impact the next seven generations."*

The story Macy tells calls for a rebirth of the role older people played in earlier times, one found in some indigenous cultures surviving today still trying to care for the Earth and generations yet to come.

This is truly a noble calling but many aging folks in our culture do not recognize the wisdom they carry, let alone what might be culturally appropriate ways of sharing it. This is new territory for most of us. Some who've toiled all their lives are exhausted, worn out. They just want to relax and enjoy themselves. Nothing wrong with that. Take all the time you need. You deserve it.

Others are fatalistic about their future. Some feel disempowered to make a difference so there is no point in trying; it's too late, and their lives are basically over. Those without a spiritual belief system may think spirituality is irrational thought, offering false hope to those not strong enough to face the uncertainties of life.

Some view the notion of purpose as beyond them, a waste of time to even think about. Others want to make a difference, want to create a meaningful legacy but don't know how or what to do. Yet most people hope that their life has meaning and that they will be remembered in a good way. Many long for a sense of continuity as well.

Everyone leaves a legacy, no matter how they lived, purposeful or not. Fruitful aging leaves a gift that says, *"I was here. My life meant something. I gave something meaningful to others who will carry on my values. I made a positive difference."*

Leaving this kind of legacy of continuity is dependent upon finding meaningful purpose for your life, one that gets you up in the morning with enthusiasm, clarity and vitality knowing what needs to be done. Fruitful aging comes from the heart, not from the ego. It gives you courage to do what is called for and passion to use your remaining time left on earth in ways that enrich your living.

The desire to create and live a meaningful legacy requires skillfully working with the storms of loss and suffering that can accompany aging. Some storms can be shattering blowing you down and mowing you over. If, however they are addressed skillfully, like buffalo who face directly into fierce blizzards, they can also be pathways to fruitful aging. It depends on what kind of relationship you create with them.

Today we know from sophisticated scientific observation tracking the interface of mind, emotion and immune system function that self-destructive, negative attitudes, toxic thoughts and feelings such as shame, guilt, learned helplessness, pathological anger and hostility, are risk factors for stroke, heart disease, and depression. We can actually measure how chronic stress weakens the body and accelerates aging of the brain and immune system.

The good news is that modern brain imaging technologies, like functional MRI's, have transformed our understanding, our story, of the mind/body/brain interaction, just as the invention of the microscope transformed biology. Knowledge of the brain has doubled in the past twenty years so that today we know the brain is alive and pulsing with an ability that a few years earlier our story did not think was possible.

Neuro-plasticity, the capacity of the brain to change in response to the stimulation of new learning and experience, and neuro-genesis, the addition of new brain cells and synaptic connections, can expand function or restore abilities diminished by disease or disuse – if we learn to use our minds skillfully.

The growing body of neuroscience research demonstrates that new life-experiences and activities that challenge our minds with mental and behavioral stimulation influence brain health in the same way physical exercise enhances physical health. I see and feel these results in my own experience of regular physical exercise and in mental exercise of learning a different language, practicing my guitar and learning to play the tenor saxophone, along with spiritual exercise that integrates mind and body, like yoga and T'ai Chi, all of which stimulate growth of new synaptic connections.

More good news about aging fruitfully is that

research shows a full array of mental functions hold up well into old age; some even get better IF, we use our minds skillfully! Turns out older brains have more information relevant to occupation or hobby, and they store more *cognitive templates* (mental outlines) of generic problems and solutions that can be accessed when facing a problem.

Our new story about the brain reinforces a key theme of this book: You can promote health and wellness in your aging process by using your mind to open your heart. Stop straining to figure life out because ultimately life is mysterious. You are never going to completely figure it all out. Instead seek to get comfortable with uncertainty and change. Stay open to life's uncontrollable mystery with respectful attention to learn how to be in good relationship with it. Seek balance and harmony, not perfection.

I invite you to explore how cultivating greater emotional and mental flexibility, adaptability and fluidity in coping with loss of control and unpredictability enhances your experience in responding successfully to the challenges of aging. You may find that strengthening your resiliency is more important than trying to hold on to stability and control over people and events.

The new story understanding about the participatory nature of mind/body wellbeing illuminates the primacy of conscious relationship with values, beliefs, vision, love, faith and meaning. All experience comes down to relationship. There isn't anything that is not about relationship so creating quality meaningful relationship with your self, with others and with the creative powers of the universe is the bottom line of living a good life as you age.

Mystical Trappist monk Thomas Merton speaks eloquently about what meaningful relationships can lead us to when they are held in the contextual story of a maturing spiritual intelligence.

"Then it was as if I suddenly saw the secret beauty of their hearts, the depths of their hearts where neither sin nor desire nor self-knowledge can reach, the core of their reality, the person that each one is in God's eyes. If only they could see themselves as they really are. If only we could see each other that way all the time, there would be no more war, no more hatred, no more cruelty, no more greed...I suppose the big problem would be that we would fall down and worship each other."

—Contemplative Prayer - Thomas Merton

Chapter Eight

Creating a Fruitful Aging Practice.

When the going gets tough,
you get what you practice.

—Unknown source

Fruitful aging is characterized by seeing and living from the heart, the result of working the five developmental challenges presented in this book. Success calls for quality attention and strengthened concentrative power, which in turn requires some kind of mindfulness practice to develop. It doesn't have to be formal meditation. It can be anything that has you paying attention to your direct experience in the moment that you keep coming back to when you lose your focus.

It can be washing the dishes, pulling weeds, vacuuming the rug. If done mindfully, using the activity to focus on the moment with careful attention, you strengthen the muscle of your mind. The next ingredient in the fruitful aging formula is careful intention.

Intention is key. Everything starts with

intention. Think about a sailboat at sea. Trained sailors don't control wave, current, weather or wind. But when they know where they want to go, i.e. intention, they can create a relationship with those forces that they can't control to help them get to where they want to go. Without clear intention or learning how to sail, the poor sailor is at the mercy of whichever direction the strongest current and tide is going at the time, which could be disastrous.

Clear intention for your life acts like a flashlight beam in a dark room showing you how to skillfully navigate the journey of your life. When you have clear intention you become like the sailor who knows where she wants to go and has the knowledge to skillfully work with forces beyond her control using greater power than her own to achieve her goals.

EXERCISE

To create your own clear intention go back and review your harvested wisdom teachings and your sense of mission and purpose. Think about the key qualities of being you would like to grow that are in alignment with your vision and values. Sit down and do some writing about this, giving free reign to whatever wants to come out. Write as much as you want without censoring it. When finished, walk away and leave it alone for awhile. Let it simmer.

When you are ready, go back and review

what you wrote. Next, synthesize the essence of what you have produced down to one or two sentences, stated only in present tense and in a positive framework. No negative wording because a single negative gives the unconscious something to pounce on and it will. Safeguard your intention and feed your unconscious only positive thoughts. For each word is a seed, a building block for a new program in your subconscious mind.

Here are some examples to get you going, the first of which reflects general qualities that apply to everyone.

"I am a sacred worthy luminous being. I am love and my love is for giving."

A second intention statement reflects specific personal qualities I am working on to enrich the fruitfulness of my life. I want to eliminate or at least reduce the opposite qualities that can take hold when my ego is in reactivity; when my reptilian brain high-jacks my cerebral cortex out of fear to fight or flee. Instead I want to grow my capacity to experience more of what the below intention statement affirms:

"I am a joyful, kind, patient, fluid-flowing, adaptable peaceful man of light and love. I am one with the universe. I am one with you."

Here is an intention statement from a young friend - *"I am a profound, courageous life-force, talented in loving myself and benevolent to all."*

As you work on your intention focus on the qualities of being you want to have be a mainstay of your life, then come up with your own intention statement reflecting your values of what is most important to you. Write down a draft copy and clarify it on paper. Try to get your intention writings down to one or two sentences, all stated present tense and positively framed Try reading it out loud. Notice how you feel.

It may seem like what you wrote is not true at but remember these words are like a flashlight beam cutting through reactive darkness to show you a safe and fruitful path to walk on. Your degree of uncomfortability with what you wrote shows you are on the right path; it shows the direction to grow in.

Next write your intention statement on a several 3 x 5 cards. Place cards somewhere in your home where you can see them on a regular basis. Put one on your bathroom mirror, on your refrigerator door. Put one in your checkbook, on your desk, on the dashboard of your car, on your computer. Carry one around with you referring to it during the day. Most important of all, start your day by taking some quiet time to repeat your intention statement very slowly and very consciously each morning soon after you wake up. Memorize it. Use it as a mantra as you go through your day.

In doing this you are creating a practice based on what you want to have more of in your life. It is especially vital to start your day by repeating your intention statement; otherwise, your conditioned software kicks in automatically without you having to push the play button. For most of us this mind software is fear-based conditioning, predicated on perception of a separate ego identity shaped significantly by preconscious inputs starting in the mother's womb and further impacted by childhood experience. This results in sensitivities or hot-spot buttons that, when pushed, respond with the programmed reactivity – anger, hurt, retreat, attack, contraction, inflammation, self-pity, depression, etc.

If you want to respond in a more skillful and fruitful manner aligned with your intention, pull the plug on the old software and activate the new one by starting to repeat it to your self when you first wake up even before you even get out of bed. Next, create an empowerment ritual to really juice up your energetic alignment with the words and meaning of your intention statement.

EXERCISE

You can use the following suggestions to create a simple ritual that works best for you.

First, create designated special or sacred space. Light a candle, burn some incense.

Then do slow belly breathing to induce your relaxation response, lowering your heart rate while opening your mind to deeper levels of connection. Ground and center yourself.

Tune into what you are truly thankful for about your life in this very moment. Think about what is the source of all that you are thankful for – Father/

Mother God, Goddess, Spirit, Nature, Ancestors, the Earth, whatever it is. Extend gratitude from your heart to that source.

This very act of giving heart-felt gratitude will open you up to positive energy. Why? Because the act of giving thanks opens your consciousness to what has always been there, cosmic support. You are not alone in the universe. Whatever your challenge, don't limit your response to trying to meet it with just ego energy, i.e., on your own. Remember your connection to the infinite energy of the universe and plug in!

The plugging in process gets stronger when you think about how you didn't create the air you are breathing or the gravity holding you to the earth so that you don't float off into space. You didn't create the sun or the trees or the plants or the plankton in the ocean using photosynthesis that enables life to exist on our planet. No, you and I are recipients of a creative wisdom power that knows how to make all this happen. Consciously plugging into this creative force vitalizes body, mind, and spirit.

Staying in gratitude, repeat your intention statement. Pay careful attention to each word. Visualize it in your mind, feel its energy. Each word is a building block in the creation of a thought pattern, a new software program, and a flashlight showing you the way to go in your life to bring about your greatest good. Repeat your intention for a good five minutes or so. Allow your self to move spontaneously into chanting or singing your intention. Allow yourself to move or dance should your body want to move. Add background music if you want. Have fun with this and know that your intention statement will change over time as your progress with your intentions.

When you are finished with the time you have allotted for your ritual, close with gratitude. Now move forward into your day to live out your intention. Make sure to carry the three by five card with you until you have memorized your intention. Take it out periodically throughout the day to reconnect with it.

*****

It also helps to program your environment with pictures, images, objects you have or can make that deepen your concentration to the meaning and significance of your intention.

One of many symbols I place around my house is pictures and figures of hummingbirds. I love their buzzing sound when I am out working in the garden, the flash of bright color on their heads when the sunlight hits them. Rainbow photographs are another. Buddha and Virgin de Guadalupe figurines are other favorite symbols. They all remind me that Spirit is always present and that I can open to it whenever I so choose. Seeing them is like a kick in the butt to live in alignment with my intention statement with which I start the day.

Take some time to see what symbols and images are inspirational for you. Be open to finding or creating new ones that arise spontaneously from your intuition. You will know them when you see them because your energy will jump up saying *"yes!"*

When you get into bed at night repeat your intention statement for a few minutes. Look back at your day to see how you did with it. See where you dropped the ball, where you forgot, or acted in an opposite way. Review without judgment or criticism but with intent to learn from the situation so you can do better the next time a similar situation comes up.

Forgive yourself if you notice judgment or faultfinding arising in your mind. Be gentle. Be compassionate. Be kind with yourself. Learn what is there to learn, congratulate yourself for your efforts to wake up, and set your resolve to use the new information as you go forward the following day. Once again, close with gratitude for whatever you are thankful about the day you have just lived. Then drift off into a good night's rest.

When you start and end your day aligning with your intention, you give yourself an incredible tool for enriching your life. When you have clear intention you can respond to any disturbance, any upset, any challenge, with this question: *"How can I create a response to this that grows me in the direction of my greatest good, the direction I want to go?"*

Like a skilled sailor you too create a response to the currents and tides of your life whereby you use them to help you go where you want to go.

Instead of being a victim of circumstances, you use circumstances and their energy they trigger to help you accomplish your goals living your intention like a surfer catching a wave.

Your practice will help you conserve, build and recharge your energy like a hybrid car at a stoplight. Set goals but be patient, remember that it takes a good 36 days to root new behaviors into enduring habits. Identify obstacles and uncover sources of resistance; problem-solve solutions. Use relapses and setbacks as learning experiences and reset goals as needed.

Fine-tune your intention statement as your goals change or you want to work on different aspects of yourself. Create a support system of family, friends, and caregivers if you have them, whomever you can enlist to support you in staying true to your intentions. You may find your example motivates others to create conscious intention and practice for their own lives. It can be catching!

By working your intention as a practice, your experience begins to change in the direction you want it to go. Starting your day by consciously connecting with your intention is an important way of loving yourself. To not do so reinforces your old reactivity patterns and creates pain and suffering.

Contrary to usual thoughts about being disciplined, this intention practice is really about growing into a more loving relationship with yourself, with others, with life itself. The more opportunities and ways that you can open your heart to the presence of love, the richer your life and your aging will be. **In the game of life, the one who loves the most wins.**

Love is about joy, something most of us would welcome more of in our lives. Happiness is different from joy. Happiness is a momentary feeling. Joy is actually an attitude toward life. You will not always be happy but you can create and live a consistent attitude of gratitude toward life, toward your existence, towards what is happening in the moment. It all comes down to your intention – what you want to experience more of in life: joy and love or fear and anxiety.

Today there is a rapidly growing social science field called positive psychology whose research shows how love, joy, compassion, gratitude, forgiveness, optimism and focusing on the positive contribute to greater physical, mental, emotional and spiritual health. A 2005 study reported in the Archives of General Psychiatry actually shows wounds heal significantly faster in loving couples than in hostile ones.

Healthy, supportive and loving relationships start with intention and are built on skillful communication, genuine caring and a willingness to put love into action by really listening to another. When your life and relationship intentions are spiritually oriented you activate movement toward the fullest realization of your highest potentials of intelligence, mature spirituality, turning the challenges of aging into opportunities for enriched living.

Mature spirituality recognizes the essential oneness of life and creation while simultaneously appreciating the unique ways the universe expresses itself through the individual diversity of your unique being. As a newborn you come into this world just being with your being. You are a *be-er*. You eat, poop, and take in experience and sleep. Gradually your nervous system matures. You learn to stand up, to walk, to talk, etc. You become a *do-er*. You define yourself and others by what you do. You meet someone at a party and ask, *"What do you do?"* You might have also heard, *"Don't just stand there, do something!"*

Take away our doings and our distractions and we get fidgety. Nervous. Anxious. We find it uncomfortable to just be. It is hard for most of us to slow down and simply be with our being. Doing nothing for a while except being. How about trying this opposite saying on for size to see how it makes you feel: *"Don't just do something, sit there and be! Be with your being."*

But what about when your *beingness* gets distracted or interrupted by someone else's *beingness*? Especially when it is someone whose *beingness* pushes your buttons! Remember our earlier discussion about the power of how we frame a situation in our mind? As an experiment you might try switching your frame about a button-pusher by saying to yourself — *"There is purpose for this person beings present in my life now because the button they are pushing is bringing up something in me that needs some attention. Perhaps it is an unacknowledged part of myself that I have been holding, repressing or projecting onto someone else. Perhaps it is an aspect of myself that needs love, compassion and tenderness. Maybe this situation is showing me a part of myself that needs forgiveness and acceptance. Perhaps what I judge in another, where it is easier to see I also judge in myself."*

How about using the situation with the button pusher to work your intention and see where you fall short? You might even try giving thanks for the button pusher showing up exactly as they are, pushing exactly the buttons they are pushing saying to yourself, — *"Maybe being with this person and feeling what I do are precisely what I need to experience to open my closed heart and come back into an awareness of love's presence. Thank you."*

An example from my life goes back to when I first met Edward to interview him as a possible treatment staff person at the drug program I was directing at the time. My first impression was that I thought he was the most arrogant, obnoxious, insensitive person I had ever met in my life. I couldn't stand him!

I didn't care for my wife's feedback that night when I told her about Edward: *"You know everything you say about him you do too sometimes."* Ouch! That wasn't fun to hear, but on closer inspection I saw she was right. I saw that it was as if Edward was holding up a mirror in which I could see my own obnoxious, arrogant and insensitive behaviors.

I gave Edward a second chance, this time without my self-righteous judgments. I resolved to try and see his light and not just his shadow. With this new awareness and intention over time I saw that he was truthful and authentic about what he thought and was feeling. Yes, he was strong in his opinions but he was actually respectful about others and their opinions. It was clear to me that I could count on him to tell me the truth. I hired him. He became one of my best friends.

Button-pushers bring an invitation to travel inward to see what might need some transformation attention in order to enrich your life. Sometimes there are hidden gifts amidst the trying circumstances, as was so interaction with Edward and my painful back injury opening my awareness to making needed changes in my foundational beliefs and approach to life.

This reframing work with button-pushers calls for a fierceness of attention toward a new way of thinking, something the Greek philosopher Plotinus suggested centuries ago: *"We must close our eyes and invoke a new manner of seeing... a wakefulness that is the birthright of us all though few put it to use."*

We can nurture a "new manner of seeing" by making time each day for quieting the mind and noticing that the most important and powerful aspects of life are invisible – the air we breathe, the wind, the love that warms our hearts, the kindness that soothes our soul.

A new way of seeing comes from trusting the presence and creative wisdom power of this invisible reality that underlies physical manifestation, call it spirit, God, Goddess, call it sacred mystery or whatever works for you. The name isn't so important. What is important is whether you are able to surrender into it peacefully letting go of attachment to how you want people and things to be. Surrendering to a mysterious invisible higher power is different from giving up. Giving up is quitting, usually with anger, frustration, blame, shame, feelings of failure. Surrender is accepting that you are not able to change this troublesome situation that is upsetting you so. Surrendering is releasing your burdens with faith into bigger hands trusting that the sacred mystery wisdom will some how, in some way that can't be seen or known at this time, deliver an outcome that is for the greatest good of all concerned. The challenge and the opportunity is to make faith an active verb by surrendering.

In the process of writing this book I set various deadlines for myself with specific time lines. By such and such a time I would have the outline written. By such and such a time I would complete the editing, etc. Yet when unexpected events beyond my control would occur, like the terminal illness of a close friend across the country, who asked me to come be there with him as he died, kept me from meeting my accomplishment goals on time I was faced with a choice. Get upset or surrender into what I call *bigger currents* of Divine Timing and Divine Order. For peace of mind I had to let go of my ego's schedule and open to spirit's schedule trusting that greatest good was working through it all.

Surrender by itself however does not guarantee greatest good outcome. Greatest good outcomes require you to show up to do your part, which in turn can open the door for the greatest good to come through. What might you be able to do in the situation that would *raise the sparks* lifting consciousness to a higher elevation?

Let me give you an example. I don't want to tell you how many times I have waited impatiently in a bank line when I am in a hurry and the person in front of me at the teller is sharing what appears to be their whole life history. Or there aren't enough tellers when the line stretches out halfway to the street. Wow, does my ego go into reactivity, making everybody wrong while sending a huge bomb of poisonous stink-energy into the field. I've been triggered. My intention trampled by my angry thoughts and feelings.

So here is how I am work with it. I reframe the whole situation: *The reason I am there feeling what I am feeling is that there are others feeling the same thing, and it is all coming out at the tellers who are just trying to do their job, probably underpaid and on the receiving end of a lot of hostility all day long. I can add to this pain and suffering or I can do my part to change it by changing around my own experience.*

I figuratively pick up the tool of my intention statement from the tool belt in my mind reminding myself that I am love and my love is for giving. I release judgment, open my heart and start sending love energy to the tellers. I send it to the person telling their life story. *Maybe this is the only human contact they have where someone will listen to them.*

I remind myself to open to divine presence, to divine order, to divine timing. I remind myself that my only task is to dissolve any thought forms of separation and wake up to oneness, knowing love's presence is here and I can enjoy it right now!

Your intention statement practice can help you stay conscious of divine connection. Sometimes it happens as a gift of grace. Yesterday in a market I passed a young woman pushing a baby carriage. I looked in to see who was there. My eyes locked in with a three-month-old baby girl. The baby's face lit up with a huge smile. So did mine. We continued there for a few minutes enjoying our connection. That little girl had a million-volt infectious smile. I turned to the mother, *"Your little girl is incredible!"*

Meeting the little girl was a gift of grace, but you can call forth grace by seeking magic in the ordinary. Give thanks for the little things you normally take for granted; standing up, walking, seeing, hearing, tasting, the ability to feel, to learn, to touch and be touched by others, by the diversity and beauty of nature and the miracles of creation. Gratitude is free, so you can't beat the price. See how the intention to carry an attitude of gratitude can up-level the quantity and quality of joy in your life, making your aging as fruitful as you want it to be.

Research at the HeartMath Institute of Boulder Creek, California shows that when you focus your intention and awareness on your heart and call up caring, appreciation and love, your heartbeat shifts into a more rhythmic pattern. This in turn activates a cascade of neural and biochemical events that reduce the stress hormone cortisol, while also producing oxytocin and DHEA hormones that promote healthier, happier and longer living.

It's in the books; science backs it up: an *"attitude of gratitude"* leads to better, sounder sleep, less anxiety and depression, higher long-term satisfaction with life, and kinder behavior toward others, including romantic partners.

Another experiment, this one at Northeastern University, Monica Bartlett and David DeSteno found that gratitude enhances empathy. It's an equal-opportunity emotion — Anyone can experience and benefit from it.

EXERCISE

Keeping a gratitude journal is a good way to add more joy to your life. Make it a point at the end of the day to list five things for which you felt grateful. It could be anything: a kind gesture from a friend or stranger, something new you learned, a sunset you've enjoyed. Write one sentence for each of the five things.

Compared with control groups, people keeping a gratitude journal were more optimistic, felt happier and reported fewer physical problems.

Gratitude works and it is not hard to do. Meister Eckhart offers a simple formula — *"If the only prayer you said in your whole life was, 'Thank You', that would suffice."*

*****

The real value of a gratitude-based intention practice is that it will raise your consciousness. Ordinary consciousness is significantly underdeveloped compared to what is possible. The gero-transcendence drive inherent in aging urges exploration of new possibilities for higher levels of consciousness and relationship suggested by the world's spiritual traditions and mystics throughout the ages.

Ordinary folk like you and I may through grace and serendipity momentarily experience higher states of a luminous nature and transpersonal being. These experiences are marked by heightened concentration, insight, positive emotional affect and felt-union with the sacred offering a glimpse of what spiritual mature looks and feels like.

While short-lived states can open the awareness-door to higher potentials the real need is to create a behavioral trait out of a transitory state. No way around it, this takes a sustained, disciplined practice such as working with an intention practice that reduces ego identification and grows the kind of spirituality that creates win-win outcomes for all life and creation.

Ego isn't bad; in fact it helps us learn how to take care of ourselves. We need it. But it is not the totality or reality of who and what we really are. It is a mental and psychological construct. Just as you wouldn't let a two-year-old drive your car down the freeway, don't allow your ego to run your life, You might be heading for a crash.

Aging fruitfully by growing mature spiritual intelligence reveals the gold of the golden years as the expansion of consciousness into identifying with the holy. Black Elk, the Lakota Sioux medicine man talking about an experience of altered consciousness in a vision puts it this way:

"Then I was standing on the highest mountain of them all, and round about beneath me was the whole hoop of the world. And while I stood there I saw more than I can tell and I understood more than I saw; for I was seeing in a sacred manner the shapes of all things in the spirit, and the shape of all shapes as they must live together like one being.

And I saw that the sacred hoop of my people was one of many hoops that made one circle, wide as daylight and as starlight, and in the center grew one mighty flowering tree to shelter all the children of one mother and one father. And I saw that it was holy."

Physicist Sir James Jeans adds a scientific perspective:

"The material world constitutes the whole world of appearance but not the whole world of reality."

Indian mystic Sri Aurobindo points out:

"The Self is that one immutable, all-pervading, all-containing, reality hidden behind our mental being into which our consciousness widens out when it is liberated from the ego."

Poet Walt Whitman contributes a poet's view:

"I am not contained between my hat and my boots."

Philosopher Arnold Schopenhauer says:

"Our apparent separateness is but the effect of the way we experience forms under the conditions of space and time. Our true reality is in our identity and unity with all life."

Luke in The New Testament 17:20-21:

"The Kingdom of God is within you."

And finally author Antoine de Saint-Exupéry in The Little Prince reminds us:

"For behind all things lies something vaster; everything is but a path, a portal, or a window opening on something more than itself.... It is only with the heart that one can see rightly; what is essential is invisible to the eye."

Chapter Nine

Recognition Rites Honoring Elders

*You must give birth to your images. They are the
future waiting to be born.*

—Rainer Maria Rilke

What happens after completion of the five fruitful
aging developmental tasks —

> *Revisioning death as an ally empowering life.*

> *Reclaiming your wisdom teachings and re-
> pairing your relationships.*

> *Realizing your heart path with vision and
> purpose.*

> *Reawakening your power of creativity, cour-
> age and generativity, and*

> *Recognizing your highest potential by grow-
> ing your spiritual maturity and intelligence?*

Now it's about an initiatory rite of passage.
The initiation rites for the first half of life are
about preparing the initiate to fulfill an adult role

in society. What's needed in the later cycle of life is a rite of passage that enables the older person to be seen and affirmed as a vital and valuable contributor to society in their new role as elder.

Traditionally rites of passage in indigenous cultures include some kind of a test so modern rites need the same dynamic to make them meaningful. Passing the test validates to the initiate and the community the emergence of a new entity presenting itself in service to their welfare.

Noting the absence of such an initiatory rite for elders in our culture I decided to create one — Recognition Rites Honoring Elders. The rite aims to shift attitudes about aging to the position of respect and reverence mature cultures have by valuing and using their older people in socially integrative ways. Here is a story I heard at a gathering of storytellers that speaks to this recognition.

The Woman and the Stone

An old woman was traveling from her village to her sister's village, a day's journey she made every month. As she stepped across the stream on the way there, she noticed something shining in the water. She stooped and picked up a magnificent stone. She knew it must be a jewel of some kind. Perhaps it had fallen from a noble's garment as he crossed the water on horseback. She put it in her lunch basket, thinking how lucky she was to find it.

A little later she sat down under a tree for lunch from her basket. A young man looking hungry and tired came down the path. She offered to share her lunch with him. She discovered, as they chatted, he was on his way to her village to find work. When she opened up her basket to put things away after lunch, he noticed the stone in the basket and asked to see it. She took it out and showed it to him. "You should take this," she said. "I found it in the stream and think it may be worth quite a lot. You may need it if you do not find work." The young man accepted her offer swiftly and they parted.

The next week, when the woman returned to her village, friends ran to greet her saying, "There is a young man who has been looking everywhere for you." When the young man found her, he took the stone from his pocket saying, "I want to return this to you."

"Why?" she asked, "Is it not worth anything?"

"Yes," he said, "it is worth a great deal. But I've found work, and I want to give it back in hope that you can give me something that is even more precious. Give me what you have within you that enabled you to give me this stone." (Spellbinders. Aspen, CO)

The Recognition Rite program I developed creates an opportunity for an older person to give a younger one what they have but first you have to help them find it. The process starts when you decide who you want to honor, someone whose life you want to celebrate. Then you share with that person what the Recognition Rite is about to gain their interest and buy in. Once that is accomplished you basically take them through the five developmental tasks to fruitful aging using the format of this book as a guide.

I initially focus on the reflection questions of Chapter Three helping the person find their wisdom teachings, repair their relationships and get a sense of what gifts they have to share that could benefit others.

If you are uncomfortable facilitating this process or if you want supportive backup material you can order a copy of Abe Arkin's *Life Workbook* which contains 14 chapters, each addressing a different reflection question along with informative reading, quotes, background theory, research results, stories and writing assignments that stimulate the natural drive of gero-transcendence.

After completing the reflection questions of mine or Abe's, both of which constitute a inner vision quest, the next step is addressing what Black Elk, the Sioux medicine man, meant when he told people returning from a quest that their vision was not complete until they had *"danced it out before the people."*

In Black Elk's time and setting this meant calling the people of the tribe into a ceremonial gathering. The returning quester, wearing clothing and decorations that symbolized the vision and gift they had received during their time in the wilderness shared a song, a dance, or some sort of ceremonial act demonstrating their new position in life with the gifts and responsibilities therein.

In our modern day setting the challenge is to create a testing initiatory rite of passage relevant to the initiate. First you help them access their creativity to find a dramatic way, *an act of power* that demonstrates their elder wisdom-gifts in a public presentation. Passage over the initiatory threshold comes through performing the act of power they came up with before invited guests. Joseph Campbell provides context:

"We are all called to be heroes within the terms and values of our lives; did we show up and give authentic self-expression and devotion to whatever calling came to us from our depths, dying to the group mythology we inherited so that we could be born again in our authenticity?"

Don Leonard, a retired 76 year-old engineer met that call. Don was depressed due to a worsening series of physical and cognitive challenges. In his earlier life he'd been a successful engineer, a very active do-er and problem-solver, someone who was always helping others with their problems. Don felt this was all in his past now. He felt old and useless, his vitality and vigor gone, no longer able to contribute to life.

Don, with my facilitation and the active support and participation of his wife Susan went through the Recognition Rites program using the reflection questions to discover and harvest his wisdom teachings. He looked into the face of his death and created a life-empowering relationship to it; he went on his inner vision quest to find a new life purpose; he accessed his creativity and courage to find an act of power by which he would come out in the world with a new identity: as an elder with something of value to share with his community. He created an intention statement and a practice to try and live it each day as best he could.

In doing this work Don deepened into his spirituality. He came to realize how alive he felt when people asked him to pray for them or their loved ones or friends. Whenever it happened he felt that he still had something of value to contribute to others. It wasn't in his old way of physically helping people because his diminishing physical abilities, decreased mobility, and short-term memory problems didn't allow for that kind of giving. None of that interfered however with his ability to connect with spirit when someone was in need of a prayer. To his delight Don found that praying for other people was his new gift that enabled him to share the love in his heart through his connection with Spirit.

He also discovered he didn't have to limit his heart sharing to when he was asked to do a prayer. He could send out his love energy anytime he wanted. He did confess, however, that he wished more people would ask him for prayers. I pointed out to Don that he needed to let people know about his availability as a prayer resource person, which the public rite of passage would be a perfect vehicle for doing.

During his work with the reflection questions Don remembered a poem from earlier in his life. He wanted to use it in some way in his rite. After talking about it with his wife a decision was made to share the poem as a song. Don enlisted the help of his wife and grandchildren to join him on a big drum, each with their own drumstick to accompany his song when the time came. Afterwards he'd talk about the wisdom lessons of his life.

How often does an older person get a chance to tell their life story these days, let alone have it be listened to by an inter-generational audience? Don was going to get that chance in his passage rite. Stepping into the spotlight would test him because it was not a place he was comfortable being in. His concluding act of power would be offering a prayer for the entire gathering.

Don was nervous knowing the rite would push him out of his comfort zone. He was basically a shy fellow who didn't like center stage. By having the courage to show up for his passage rite he'd be simultaneously demonstrating his prayer gift while also letting people know he was plugging back into life with a new way of contributing.

Preparing for the rite was already raising Don's self-esteem and shifting his self-image from that of a useless non-contributor to a new and positive valuation of himself. He was beginning to see himself as an elder who understands the value of deep being and who offers himself in service to his community from that place.

Don came up with a list of people from his life that he wanted to attend his rite. Each person was invited to *"A Recognition Rite Honoring the Life of Don Leonard"* and asked to come prepared to share how knowing Don had impacted their lives.

A hall was rented for the event. It was decorated with a montage of pictures from different times of Don's life, along with artwork and symbols that were meaningful to Don. His favorite music was playing in the background as almost one hundred people arrived from all around the country.

The afternoon of the event I acted as emcee on Don's behalf welcoming everyone and setting the context by briefly explaining the ideas behind the program. Stepping back I then opened the stage for family and friends in the audience to stand up and share their stories about Don. This is a wonderful opportunity for the honoree to hear what otherwise might only be shared at their memorial service after they have died. This way they get to be present and hear how their life has impacted others.

As it was for Don, this sharing is deeply touching for all. Poignant and humorous stories brought forth tears, laughter, memories rekindled of shared adventures and mis-adventures.

The proceedings were videotaped so Don and his family could take in all of what happened at their leisure after the event was over. They could also share it with family and friends not able to be there in person. There was also a photographer taking candid photos, which resulted in a color, hardbound memory book, a keepsake for generations to come.

After family and friends finished sharing their memories with Don it was time for Don's act of power, his testing threshold. He stood up, balanced himself on his cane, thanking everyone for being there. He shared a brief, highlighted narrative of his life, including the major and most meaningful events emphasizing what he learned from them. He then spoke about his aging challenges and how he saw himself in a new and positive light with something of worth to share, which he was going to do through a ritual.

Don had his family come forward onto the stage to drum together on the large drum. Afterwards he conducted a prayer service that enfolded everyone in a sharing of his love and appreciation. He told everyone he was henceforth available for anyone who needed a supportive prayer. That was his gift, giving love to others by connecting with spirit through prayer.

The event ended with everyone standing up, holding hands and singing the poem- song that expressed Don's feelings about the stage of life he was entering.

> *It's enough to be alive today*
> *to see the sea and sky*
> *to watch the changes come and go*
> *to love without asking why.*
> *It's enough to be alive today*
> *To eat, joke, create and relate*
> *No longer needing to be somebody*
> *Now I can just be me.*

*****

"We become what we display," says religious historian Mircea Eliade. In Don's rite of passage experience he was seen, heard and affirmed through his display. You can watch a 10-minute video of highlights from Don's Recognition Rite event at my website: drtompinkson.com.

As much as Don benefitted from the

recognition rite his display allowed listeners in the audience to benefit as well in both seeing and hearing something that came from his soul. This is important for as anthropologist Barbara Meyerhoff recognized from her study of aging members in a senior center in Los Angeles there is a tragic loss in *"not seeing and listening"* to soulful sharing. She calls for a *"partnership of soul"* in which both the speaker who is heard and seen and listeners who hear and see grow their souls together.

Meyerhoff believes there is a fundamental healing that takes place when a personal life story is told and heard for it furthers moral and spiritual growth which *"is the main goal and fruit of living a long life, no small compensation in extreme old age."*

Don't underestimate the power of this kind of shared experience of storytelling and listening. *"The word moves a bit of air and this the next"*, says Rabbi Nachman of Bratslav, a wisdom elder from the 19th century, *"until it reaches the one who receives it, and he receives his soul therein, and therein is awakened."*

After Don's rite of passage was over, guests and family lingered for quite some time enjoying food and drink together. Listening in on conversations I heard many people commenting how touched they were by what had taken place, how it changed their minds about aging and older people, how it gave them a new perspective on their own aging.

Especially moving was Don's demonstration

that the content of his being was more important and defined more of who he truly was then the aging, changing form of his physical body. Don's glowing countenance was ample proof of his newfound pride, happiness and enhanced self-esteem and self-worth. He successfully modeled converting aging challenges into opportunity to grow a new sense of identity and purpose.

I did a follow-up session with Don and his wife Susan a week after the event and they were still riding a wave of joy. He is a wonderful example of surrender to what is: while keeping an open heart to new ways of being when the old ways no longer are possible.

As with Don's Recognition Rite, recognition rites can bring people of diverse background and belief systems together for an event that helps break down barriers of separation between races, ages, religions and social class. They nurture community. They foster greater appreciation of older people and how love and appreciation enriches all our lives. People's hearts are touched planting a stimulus seed to create meaningful celebrations for significant elders in their own lives.

Yet many people do not have meaningful and supportive community, family or friends in their lives as did Don. All too many elders live alone and struggle with loneliness and isolation. Putting together a Recognition Rite for such elders provides a vehicle to bring people together to form a temporal community for the event itself.

It is an opportunity to think about significant people in your life creating a stimulus to renew and reconnect with people not seen or been in touch with for years.

If you or an older person are living alone without significant others, the occasion of planning a Recognition Rite event can also be a stimulus to seek out new relationships and connections, who might find the event to be of interest for their own lives. Check out what kind of social support services there are for older people in the area where you live. Talk to your doctor, a social worker at a social service agency, a senior citizen facility, the YMCA or YWCA, your local church, synagogue, or mosque. They might have some ideas or know other older people who might also be interested in a recognition rite.

Get to know new folks. When the time is right, let them know about the planned for Recognition Rite. You never know how it could be a magnet for bringing new people together into an experience that enriches them all. Life is an exploration of what is possible and fruitful aging is always possible no matter where you live or the challenging conditions in which you live.

Speaking of challenging conditions, on a recent visit with Don a year later he shared candidly that he is facing a challenge many of us fear – Alzheimer's. In the time from when I had last seen him Don had been going downhill with increasingly painful, debilitating physical challenges and worsening short-term memory loss leading to the recent diagnosis of Alzheimer's.

Susan now makes daily to-do lists for Don to give him a structure for his day. When he walks into a room and forgets why he is there, he gets frustrated. He gets angry. But then he goes back to where he came from and finds Susan's instruction sheet that helps get him back on track. Don sees that it is hard on Susan and that makes him sad. It's asking for trouble to leave Don alone now. He forgets there is something on the stove cooking, so Susan has enlisted friends to come by and be with Don on a weekly basis so she can get away for errands or time alone to take care of herself.

Despite his travail, he forgets what he said a moment ago and repeats him self, Don continues to shine when you are with him. He is loving, thoughtful, kind, peaceful, funny, observant and sharp in the moment. *"How do you do it, Don?"* I ask. *"How do you stay positive? What helps you to be in good relationship with what is happening to you?"*

In a self-effacing manner he shrugs. *"Not fighting or resisting what is happening. I know what I have lost. I know what I can't do anymore and that makes me sad. But there is still a lot I can do and that I enjoy – 'puttering' around the house, enjoying nature, music, friends. Loving Susan. She takes such good care of me.*

I let go of what I can't do any longer and focus on what I can do and enjoy that. I have a lot of gratitude for my life. It's been really good and I am so thankful. I love just being and sharing my love with others. I think that is why I am here – to share love until my life is over and I go back to Spirit."

Impressed by Don's equanimity, I wanted to know what underlies his faith and trust. *"How does your spirituality play into this, Don?"* He pondered this for a few moments. Then he looked up at me with a gentle smile.

"I trust Spirit knows what it is doing and I just release to it. I accept my decline knowing its part of a natural process. I surrender into whatever is happening. I just keep doing what I always do, giving thanks for the blessings of my life, for Susan, my family, friends and community. I know I am in good hands. I know there is more to me than my body, which is slowly fading away. I know that this consciousness is only a small part of what really exists. I just trust Great Spirit's presence always and want to enjoy whatever I can do, and whoever is with me at the time. That makes me happy. That's it."

Anthropologist Barbara Meyerhof's study at the Senior Center in Los Angeles, underlines the dynamics of Don's recent work as it relates to the subjects she interviewed. She notes how those who age well know how to intensify the present and deepen satisfaction in small rewards and pleasures, how they are adept at providing new standards and desires as old ones became unattainable, and how they generate appropriate measures of accomplishment and worth. It's a continual process of discarding and creating, continual learning and adapting to change.

In her respondents' words:

"The task of life is to become whole," to be alive every minute, to make of suffering something positive because it is part of human life."

*****

"In old age we get a chance to find out what a human being is, how we could be worthy of being human, to find in yourself courage and know that you are vital. To do this you got to use your brain, but that's not enough. The brain is combined with the soul... I don't think you can get to this understanding too young, but when you get to it, then you couldn't go before your time, because you are ready."

*****

"Who of us can afford to overlook the lessons of the heart? How do you get a heart of wisdom mentioned in the psalms where it says – 'Teach us to number our days that we may get us a heart of wisdom?' It's in the end the only thing that gives you a good life."

*****

"We have to elevate everything to make it human, and finally you elevate the human to God...to make God's world elevated is our job. To bring it to the highest level, to a good world, a holy world. We have the power to change things, to become holy. We have to do it with the proper thoughts."

*****

These quotes and the wisdom that Don shares and lives are testimony to the gifts older people have to offer when they are recognized and honored. I hope reading about the program I developed will spur you on to finding and living your wisdom and perhaps creating your own version of programs that do so for elders in your life as well.

I love the sentiment George Bernard Shaw shares about aging fruitfully when he says –

"I rejoice in life for its own sake. Life is not a brief candle to me. It is a sort of splendid torch which I have got hold of for the moment and I want to make it burn as brightly as possible before handing it on to future generations."

Chapter Ten

Fullest Blossoming for Greatest Good

"We are all born for love; it is the principle of existence and its only end."
—Benjamin Disreali, Prime Minister
under Queen Victoria

Looking back over my many adventurous sojourns with the Huichol, one comes to mind with particular sweetness. It's about blossoming. My fellow pilgrims and I were walking slowly in a scattered group in the remote vast desert below Real de Catorce in back-country Mexico. Hot, unrelenting sun poured down from a cloudless sky. Fasting. No water. Physically weak. Trying to be spiritually strong. Each pilgrim sought the sacred cactus, peyote that Huichols have used ceremonially for centuries to open the *nierica*, the doorway of the mind to transpersonal states of consciousness to commune with the world of the spirits.

Over the long hours of scanning the ground to find the cacti, which grow flat on the ground and blend perfectly with the earth, each pilgrim found a share of the revered plant. The Huichols consider peyote a sacrament, alive, an elder, the spiritual footprint of their tribal totemic animal, the deer. Loading up my bag with bounty, I was startled by a sight I had never witnessed before: a large peyote with a delicate delightfully colored tiny flower blooming right in its center. The flower was vibrating rainbow light! My heart swelled with joyful gratitude for the gift of being able to see such numinous beauty.

Dropping to my knees I thanked the plant for its life. I offered purified sage and corn meal as a gift to its spirit. I reverently cut off the top two inches leaving the majority of its body still in the ground (its bones) so it could regenerate. Standing up to full height I held the sacred plant over my heart. *"Thank you Holy Spirits of this Holy Land. Thank you for this amazing gift. Please show me how to best honor it."* An elder noticed what I held. She came over to offer her guidance. *"Eat it. Take the flower into your heart."* So I did.

Hours later, sitting in circle around the Sacred Fire with the other pilgrims and leading shamans, it was easy to rest in silent meditation, eyes closed, exhausted but exhilarated at the same time. After awhile rainbow lights began to flash on and off beneath my eyelids. I watched them dance and dart until suddenly they coalesced into the image of a beating heart. I knew immediately that it was my heart.

In the center the tiny flower I had eaten earlier in the day appeared. Pulsating waves of rainbow light flowed from its delicate being. Watching in delight I was startled when all of a sudden it divided into two. Now two flowers pulsated waves of warm rainbow light. *"Wow, this is incredible!"*

The show was just getting started. The two flowers then divided into two more making four in all, each pulsating with the beautifully colored light. Then they just took off with exponential speed. A tidal wave of beautiful, multiplying flowers filled my heart to overflowing. I was thrilled. I thought it might stop there. But no, the flowers kept multiplying. There was no more room in my heart! *"What is going to happen now?"* I mumbled out loud.

In awe-filled rapture I watched as my heart dissolved and the pulsating flowers of light began streaming into my chest cavity, then through my entire torso until my whole body was filled with this incredible experience of blossoming flowers of beauty and bliss. The flowers spoke: *"We give this to you so you can see, feel and know what it is like when your heart is open to the existence of infinite, unconditional love. Send these flowers out to your family, your friends, and your fellow pilgrims. Send them out into the world. Send them out to everybody. This is what life is all about. This is what you are here for! This is the true treasure, the true gold. Everything else is a dream."*

Mystics throughout time and culture say our material world of appearances is but a dream. As children we heard this wisdom when we sang the popular tune, *"Row, row, row your boat, gently down the stream. Merrily, merrily, merrily, merrily, life is but a dream."*

I am not saying it is a dream, I am not saying it is not a dream. But just to cover the odds, let's imagine that it is a dream. Then why not dream big, dream deep, dream rich? I think we have all dreamed enough nightmares. Let's dream a healing dream, a joy and beauty dream, one in which you are the hero/heroine, bringing through the highest expression of your potential in being here.

Here's my dream:

"May All Beings live in peace, freedom and justice with kindness, light and love, with food, clothing, shelter, health care, meaningful education and gainful employment opportunities, a wisdom society of sisters and brothers living together in sustainable, healthy harmony for a win-win world for all. With Your Grace, may I show up to do my part, to live fully, make a positive difference Walking in Oneness and Raising the Sparks with joy and gratitude."

*****

Dream with clear intention for your fullest blossoming and greatest good of your inner flowers. Then do your best to live it out. Do your spiritual homework, shifting identity from an ego–based relationship into a cosmic-based one in attunement with creation and creator, whatever that is for you. Dissolve self-importance, attachment, entitlement. Co-create fruitful relationship with whatever comes your way, even if it feels like crap. Create a relationship to it that transforms it into compost to fuel fruitful flowering.

It's all about relationship. There is nothing that is not about relationship. Years ago a chant came to me while fasting on vision quest in the mountains that sums it all up quite nicely:

"It's all about relationship, the web we weave so fine. It's all about relationship, the love we have to shine!"

*****

EXERCISE

Having come this far I invite you now to reflect once again on your relationship to your experience of aging What kind of relationship do you have towards and with your body? To your soul? To your family? your friends, to strangers? To your fears? To the creative powers of the universe that give you life? Pick up your journal to record what ever comes up in your thoughts.

*****

As the material presented in this book shows, those who are in good relationship with higher levels of meaning and purpose and in meaningful positive relationship with self and others shine in their quality of life. They also fight off infections better than those who do not have these factors going for them, those who have not learned to use their minds to open their hearts to the healing transformational power of unconditional love. Yet even with this qualities going for you, aging can still bring formidable challenges to anyone.

A recent book by Susan Jacoby, *"Never Say Die: The Myth and Marketing of the New Old Age,"* soberly notes that most people who live beyond their mid-eighties can expect a period of extended disability before they die. Anyone who lives beyond the age of 85 has about a fifty-fifty chance of winding up in a nursing home, just as he or she has a fifty-fifty chance of developing dementia. Ouch!

The good news here is that research shows the impact of these challenging situations is lessened for those whose life focus is on purpose-driven, meaningful activities and relationships. In other words, even in the midst of the most demanding challenges, you can still stay in a good place mentally and emotionally if your focus isn't on physical conditions but on *"other realities,"* especially spiritual ones. The sense of meaning and purpose does not have to change due to ailment or condition, only the means of expressing it changes.

Meaning and purpose are not static, solid or permanent qualities, something to obtain and keep. They evolve out of relationship and ongoing interaction with others, with ourselves and with that which is greater than our individual ego concerns. Meaning and purpose grow out of seeking to create an integral alignment between values and behavior – living out what you believe and thereby growing into harmony with your deeper self. The New Testament offers counsel in this regard in Romans 12:2:

"Do not be conformed to this world, but be transformed by the renewing of your minds so that you may discern what is the will of God."

I believe aging fruitfully entails *renewing of the mind* towards the realization that the will of God means sharing love with all, in all relationships, right up to the very end of life in our bodies. The gift of longevity is for the alchemical transmutation of life's wisdom teachings into the real gold of knowing and living the love that we are. Fullest blossoming. Greatest good. Raising the sparks. Shining Light. Finding the gold. Fruitful aging.

Recently attending my 50th high school reunion brought me back into relationship with an elementary school friend with whom I had grown up in Garrett Park, Maryland. My friend Tom was now lying in a hospital bed suffering the final ravages of ALS, Lou Gehrig's disease. Barely breathing with the help of an oxygen mask, his family and friends gathered around him, he wanted out. He had had enough suffering. His quality of life was shot. He wanted to take off the oxygen mask and just end it. He wasn't afraid of death. He felt ready to go.

His family prevailed on him to wait for the arrival of his younger brother, who was flying from the east coast to Portland, Oregon, where Tom lived. He agreed to wait but wasn't happy about it. I talked with Tom about doing a releasing ceremony prior to removal of the mask. Chris, a minister and mutual friend of ours from high school, would do a prayer. I'd lead the family and friends in a saying goodbye ritual in which each person who wished could say their final words to Tom. Then I'd play my ceramic flute as the mask was taken off and Tom went into his dying. Tom liked this format and nodded his assent.

The next day when all were gathered we did the releasing ceremony. It was a touching time for us all. The mask came off. Tom's labored breathing grew weaker. I thought of a prayer I had read in a Hindu holy book, the Ashtavakra Samhita - *"Waves of individual selves according to their nature rise up, playing for a time, and disappear. I remain the shoreless ocean."*

I put down my flute. Silence filled the room except for Tom's weak breathing. We all sent our love to him as his spirit slowly struggled to leave his body. While watching his struggle to release I imagined myself in Tom's body going through what he was undergoing right before my eyes. Immediately a question arose: *"Does my current practice serve me in staying peaceful with an open heart under this kind of challenge?"* As I sat there reflecting on this, someone started to sing Amazing Grace.

Slowly everyone started singing together, hesitatingly at first, then louder. Momentum picked up. Moments passed. Tom did a final shudder. He *died*. He finished. He graduated with grace. His spirit released back into the shoreless ocean of infinite being. Big sigh. Let him go. Warm tears trickle down my checks.

The question from a few moments ago arose again: *Does my practice serve me to go through what Tom just did, releasing into the mystery of death with a peaceful mind and open heart?*

Does yours? Now is the time to fine-tune your intention, your practice. Make it work for you. Get ready for what is to come but make sure to enjoy now. It is all we ever have!

FIND YOUR GOLD

LET IT SHINE

FULLEST BLOSSOMING

GREATEST GOOD

Closing Prayer

May I, You - All Beings
Be safe from harm
May all beings be healthy, strong and vital
May all beings prosper
May all beings be happy, peaceful and secure

*May all beings be at ease in mind and
life
May all beings age fruitfully
May all beings know how much they
are loved
That we are love
That our love is for giving
May all beings co-create and live in a
Sustainable
Peaceful
Just
Beautiful and
Harmonious world.
May it be so and may each of us show
up to do our part to make it be so!*

*With great gratitude for our shared,
sacred, being-ness
I thank you for this day.
I thank you for right now.
I thank you for the Peace of Patience
and the Patience of Peace.
I Remember and Honor that I Am Your
Child, Sired by Light and Truly Loved.
I Place My Future in Your Hands and
Choose to Experience Inner Peace
Now - Peace of Mind, Peace of Body,
Peace of Being
Feeling Joined, Connected and One
With You Who Have Been Always, Who
Will Be All-Ways, and Who Are Here
Now*

and
All who have
All who do
and All Who Will cross my path
Seeing their light, Being a Love-Finder
and a Love-Giver
Opening my heart to know the sweet
honey of your unconditional light and
love
Being a channel for it out into the
world.

Appendix

Mantras

Power Tools for Waking-Up in Daily Life Challenges. Repeat as necessary

* *When the Going Gets Tough, You Get What You Practice*

* *Love is the key, Let the Medicine Do Me*

* *I Remember and Honor that I Am Your Child, Sired by Light and Truly Loved*

* *I Place My Future in Your Hands and Choose to Experience Inner Peace Now*

* *It's All About Relationship*

* *Your Infinite Light and Love is What I See, It is a Reflection of the Light and Love in Me*

* *Thank You For This Day*

* *Thank You For Right Now*

* *My life has Abundance of Grace and the Grace of Abundance*

* *I Affirm the Drawing Power of Divine Love*

*as my Magnet for Constantly Increasing Sup-
ply*
* *I remember the Peace of Patience and the
Patience of Peace*
* *Life is an Exploration of What is Possible*

Music and Song

Soothe and inspire the soul with your favorite
ones with one of the oldest and most effective
means of safely altering consciousness, opening
the heart and connecting with spirit.

CDs by the author.

Jumping into the Real: Songs for the Soul.
Available from CD Baby at: http://www.cdbaby.
com/cd/tomas22

Sacred Ceremonial Heart Songs and Chants.
Available from Tom Pinkson 710 C St. #211 San
Anselmo, CA 94901 for $20.

Keep a Gratitude Journal. Start and end
each day with an Attitude of Gratitude, noting
three things you are thankful for, and give thanks.

**Create an Ancestor Altar to Keep the
Connection Alive.** Decorate it with beauty,
placing photographs of the generations of your
family on it in a location that is easily visible. Take
some time on a regular basis to connect with your
loved ones and "*feed them*" with appreciation,
song, flowers or whatever your heart guides you

to do. This keeps the doorway of relationship open and connected for mutual benefit of the living and those who have crossed.

Create a Sacred Sanctuary in your home; a special place for meditation, prayer, reflection, relaxing, just being. Bring nature inside — special rocks, interesting pieces of wood, plants, flowers and whatever other natural elements call to your spirit. Include inspiring figurines, photography and meaningful artwork, yours and others. This is the place to do your intention practice, your healing, your thanks-giving. This is your place of refuge. Your holy place.

Fruitful Aging Resources

The Conscious Aging Alliance

SAGE-ING ® INTERNATIONAL (the new name for the former Sage-ing Guild) is an organization with the mission of helping to change our society's current belief system from aging to sage-ing—that is, from simply becoming old to aging consciously. Sage-ing is both a philosophy and a set of psychological and spiritual practices, originally developed by Zalman Schachter Shalomi, that support living with passion, purpose, community support, inner growth and commitment to service as we age. We train and support a network of Sage-ing Leaders who transmit the wisdom of Sage-ing ® through workshops, webinars and other educational and personal growth programs. We also facilitate intergenerational service projects and support a growing network of Elder Wisdom Circles. Through our website, we offer a free six-month Membership which provides access to valuable resources for individuals wanting to do their own conscious aging work while encouraging others to do likewise.

www.sage-ing.org

Sage-ing Leader Certification Program

This is our one-year, in-depth training program which prepares people to teach Sage-ing principles and practice in their communities. For more details or to apply for the next program, contact Jeanne Marsh at 214-660-3699

SECOND JOURNEY is a social-change organization helping birth a new vision of the rich possibilities of later life…

- to open new avenues for individual growth and spiritual deepening
- to birth a renewed ethic of service and mentoring in later life
- to create new model communities—and new models OF community—for later life, and
- to marshal the distilled wisdom and experience of elders to address the converging crises of our time

Captured in the shorthand of our logo…. *Mindfulness, Service and Community in the Second Half of Life.*

www.secondjourney.org

ITINERARIES is the quarterly publication which Second Journey has been proudly producing since 2005. Featuring articles by thought leaders in the conscious aging field, Itineraries is available online at no charge. The focus of the quarterly issues varies. All four issues published in 2011 explored THE SPIRITUALITY OF LATER LIFE. CREATING COMMUNITY IN LATER LIFE was the focus of issues released in 2012. ***Odysseys for the Soul: Travel and Transformation***, released at the beginning of 2013, focused on elder travel; forthcoming issues will explore "films for the second half of life" and "practices of late-life spirituality.

Notable among our current list of eight publications is ***Aging in Community***, edited by Janice Blanchard, and ***The Spiral of the Seasons*** by John Sullivan, Second Journey's "philosopher in residence." A new book, ***Journeys Outward, Journeys Inward: Travel and Transformation***, expanded from the earlier issue of Itineraries and edited by sculptor/writer Penelope Bourk, will be released in January. Scheduled for release later in the fall are two other new books: Integral Living by John Sullivan and Second Journeys: The Call of Spirit in Later Life, edited by Bolton Anthony. Go to our Bookstore: www.secondjourney.org/bookstore.

THE ELDER SPIRITUALITY PROJECT of SPIRITUALITY AND PRACTICE provides resources for elders' spiritual journeys through SpiritualityandPractice.com, a multifaith website with a large wisdom archive containing articles on spiritual practices; book, film, and audio reviews; book excerpts; profiles of spiritual teachers; small group programs; collections of quotations, and more. The Project launched in 2013 with a series of interactive e-courses led by spiritual teachers known for their insights into the spiritual blessings and challenges of later life. To keep the e-courses affordable and easily accessible, they are delivered by email. Participants then create virtual communities in the online "Practice

Circles" where they share their experiences. The Elder Spirituality Project will be expanded in the fall of 2013 with a special section of the website for curated content, including program plans for small groups of elders in different settings; reviews of recommended books, DVDs, and audios for and about elders; and a database of quality-of-life spiritual practices for elders from all religions and spiritual paths.

www.SpiritualityandPractice.com/ElderSpirituality

Brussat@SpiritualityandPractice.com

E-Courses in the Elder Spirituality Series
E-Courses available on-demand

"Becoming a Wise Elder with Angeles Arrien" Read more about it and sign up here:

www.SpiritualityandPractice.com/ESP-BecomingaWiseElder

"The Sage's Tao Te Ching with William Martin"

Read more about it and sign up here:

www.SpiritualityandPractice.com/ESP-SagesTaoTeChing

RECOGNITION RITES FOR A NEW VISION OF AGING – HONORNG ELDERS is a program founded by **Dr. Tom Pinkson** that shifts attitudes about aging and older people to the position of respect and reverence that mature cultures demonstrate with their valuation and socially integrative use of their elders. It offers a unique blend of ancient and contemporary knowledge that is the result of Dr. Pinkson's forty years of work bridging cultures, traditions, belief systems and peoples. Recognition Rites bring people of diverse background and belief systems together for a ceremonial honoring of a selected elder that helps break down barriers of separation between races, ages, religions and social class. They build community. They foster greater appreciation of diversity, of older people, of how love and appreciation enrich all our lives. Recognition Rites serve as a seed and stimulus for others in attendance to create celebrations for meaningful elders in their own lives.

www.tompinkson.com

NATIONAL CENTER FOR CREATIVE AGING (NCCA) was founded in 2001 and is dedicated to fostering an understanding of the vital relationship between creative expression and healthy aging and to developing programs that build on this understanding. The process of aging is a profound experience marked by increasing physical and emotional change and a heightened search for meaning and purpose. Creative expression is important for older people of all cultures and ethnic backgrounds, regardless of economic status, age, or level of physical, emotional, or cognitive functioning. The arts can serve as a powerful way to engage elders in a creative and healing process of self-expression, enabling them to create works that honor their life experience.

www.creativeaging.org

ghanna@creativeaging.org

MEMORIAL BRAINWORKS is a department within Memorial Hospital of South Bend, Indiana, and an affiliate of Beacon Health System. Our philosophy is that brain health is the single most determining factor in how we live. The quality of how our mind functions drives the ability to remember, learn, relate, think, experience, contribute and enjoy life like we want today and for all of our tomorrows. Making brain-healthy lifestyle choices is an investment in long-term mind and body resilience.

Our *Sage-ing Center*, one of the vitality programs offered through the BrainWorks Wisdom School, is devoted to promoting understanding of how personal growth and development can continue as we grow older. We do this by providing webinars and, by invitation, on-site educational programs around the country.

One of our best known services is our weekend program, offered at sites across North America, to train *Sage-ing Circle Facilitators*. We also reach out to younger people to encourage lifestyles that will support healthy aging in their years ahead.

We want people of all ages to know that there is an upside to aging.

www.memorialbrainworks.com

574-647-6628   brainworks@memorialsb.org

Upcoming Webinars -see our website.

The Heart of Aging with Wisdom and Vitality: Sage-ing Circle™ Facilitator Training Program results in certification, for professionals and lay leaders seeking practical skills in leading groups and supporting individuals in cultivating their wisdom and identifying their contribution and legacy. In this three-day training program, participants receive a manual which provides them with material to teach twelve, 2-hour sessions on a variety of topics   CEU's are available. Sept. 27-29 in Kansas City, Missouri and October 25-27 In South Bend, Indiana. For information, call Rosemary Cox at 574-647-6632.

Grandbuddies: A Multigenerational Brain Health Program was the 2013 MindAlert Award winner through American Society on Aging and the MetLife Foundation. A how-to manual is available. See our website for details.

THE MANKIND PROJECT ELDERS (MKP) is made up of hundreds of members over age 50 who have formally declared themselves as elders. The mission of the elder body of the Mankind Project is to "awaken and nurture intentional eldering by teaching and mentoring." When a member becomes a "declared elder" he is announcing to the community that he is living the second half of life intentionally, and that this intention includes being a source of blessing, an advocate for Earth, a mentor and a wisdomkeeper. We accomplish our mission through annual Elder Gatherings, a series of classes called "The Elder Journey," support groups and new member initiation weekends.

http://elders.mkp.org

There are 26 Mankind Project communities across the United States. Each has elder initiation as part of their New Warrior Training initiation weekends. Visit our website to learn more.

THE LIFE PLANNING NETWORK is a community of professionals and organizations from diverse disciplines dedicated to helping people navigate the second half of life. Our mission is to create and communicate knowledge and resources that support professionals in their work to enhance people's later lives and thus benefit society.

There are several ways we support professionals in this field, including workshop leaders and facilitators. Our members can promote their organizations and activities to the public through a directory on our web site. We also list a broad range of resources specifically for our members on our web site. Members gather in chapters as they emerge around the country as well as in regular program opportunities, including teleseminars, to share and learn.

www.lifeplanningnetwork.org

Free Teleseminar Series:
Throughout the year the Life Planning Network offers a series of teleconference meetings and webinars presented by experts, many of whom are LPN members. These are designed to inform and empower members regarding developments in our fields as well as resources and best practices. All of these events are available as a benefit of membership, with non-members invited to participate in one teleconference as a way to experience LPN. You can learn about upcoming teleconferences and webinars on our website.

Announcing our e-book:
We proudly announcing the availability of our e-book, *Live Smart After 50: The Experts Guide to Life Planning for Uncertain Times.* Created by a diverse team of LPN members, this book offers eleven compelling chapters offering various perspectives on planning for the second half of life. Visit the book's website, **www. livesmartafter50.com** to learn more about the book and the recognition it is receiving, and to order.

THE LEGACY OF WISDOM project, based in Switzerland, is dedicated to creating a vision with practical applications of "wise living and aging." A growing library (200+) of "video answers to key questions" from some of our most respected generation leaders is available in our archive library. We keep it simple, limiting interviews to just 22 questions in five main areas of aging: Mission and Fulfillment; Aging Lifestyles and Relationships; Health and Healthcare; Legal and Finances; End of Life Preparations.

Legacy of Wisdom also publishes its findings from conferences and workshops with inspiring elders which we sponsor. Global in perspective and multi-generational in reach, we know that living wisely can occur at all ages. Courses for the United States are currently being developed for 2014. We welcome visits to our library, Comments and suggestions are always welcome and valued

www.legacyofwisdom.org

GRAY IS GREEN is a national non-profit focused on the possibility for older adult Americans to offer distinctive benefits to our society in response to unprecedented ecological challenges. These benefits may range from block-votes for a variety of policy changes to mass market demands for sustainable living choices in housing, food, transportation, healthcare and urban design. Gray-Greens possess unique gifts for adaptive response. Such include a wealth of *generational* responses to war, economic collapse, epidemics, and political upheaval, together with *individual* responses to parenting, managing businesses, leading organizations, voting, volunteering, meeting worklife challenges, enjoying the wonders of nature and culture, and more. Following decades of environmental change—for better and for worse—and now witnessing the cumulative environmental legacy modern society is leaving to our children and grandchildren, Gray-Greens hear the call to action and reflection.

We invite to our network individuals and organizations open to the distilled wisdom and environmental passion of older adults. In response to the longing for authentic inter-generational accountability expressed by Gray-Greens, we help foster a beneficial response. All are invited to sign up at **http://grayisgreen.org** for our periodic email updates and news items for sustainable living and environmental advocacy. The site also offers unrestricted access to our archive of information resources and a link for donors. **kathschomaker@grayisgreen.org**

FIERCE WITH AGE, The Online Digest of Boomer Wisdom, Inspiration and Spirituality is a free digest featuring daily and bi-weekly summaries and excerpts of the best writing about spirituality and aging for Boomers on the web. Editor-in-chief Carol Orsborn, Ph.D., a Boomer generation expert with a doctorate in religion and author of 21 books, cites the growing number of websites and books on the subject, as well as the increasing visibility of spiritual content on Boomer, aging and spirituality websites. Fierce with Age offers self-guided online retreats on the subject of spirituality and aging.

www.fiercewithage.com for information and to subscribe **carol@fiercewithage.com**

Carol Orsborn's memoir about spirituality and aging: *Fierce with Age: Chasing God and Squirrels in Brooklyn* is available through Amazon. com.

On October 1st, the Fierce with Age microsite will be officially launched on Beliefnet.com, the comprehensive multi-faith online resource for inspiration and spirituality. Readers can find articles from Beliefnet columnist Carol Orsborn at **http:www.beliefnet.com/Wellness/Fierce-with-Age/index.aspx**

THE CENTER FOR CONSCIOUS ELDERING, The Center for Conscious Eldering, based in Durango, Colorado, is dedicated to supporting the development of conscious elders. We do this by offering our signature *Choosing Conscious Elderhood* rite of passage retreats, introductory workshops by invitation from churches, retreat centers and other groups, *Coaching for Conscious Living* and *Meeting*

Ancient Wisdom pilgrimages to meet indigenous elders. We serve those in and approaching the elder third of life who seek passion, purpose, growth and service as they age. An important aspect of our uniqueness is that we use the power of nature to support your growth as an elder. It is in the natural world that we can most easily remember that which is authentic and natural in ourselves, and thus gain clarity and vision for how we can best thrive and contribute in a world urgently in need of the wisdom and gifts of *conscious* elders. Our retreats, workshops and pilgrimages all involve significant time spent outdoors in inspiring natural settings.

Upcoming Choosing Conscious Elderhood retreats and Weekend Workshops

www.centerforconsciouseldering.com

WAKAN is a spiritually based, non-profit shamanic organization & community dedicated to restoring the sacred in daily life based on indigenous wisdom teachings. The word *"Wakan"* means *sacred* in the Lakota language and *"heart of the sky"* in the Mayan language. The organization was founded by Dr. Tom Pinkson after the guidance to start a community helping people live in balance with the web of life came through on Christmas Eve, 1983.

The Assignment: *Before her death my Huichol spiritual grandmother Guadalupe de la Cruz, charged me with bringing the teachings of her People to 'El Norte' where she said we had forgotten how to live. Entering my sixty-eighth year I feel a responsibility, both as a grandfather and a citizen of Mother Earth, to pass on what I have been so fortunate to be given by my Elders. I walk my path with a firm commitment to the work of bringing forth indigenous wisdom to address the problems of contemporary society. Wakan is one vehicle by which I seek to carry out my assignment. Wakan received tax-exempt status in 1987 and has been providing services ever since.*

How We Do It: Wakan offers teachings and tools for living in sacred oneness with the web of life, each other, and future generations through services based on indigenous wisdom of seasonal retreats, quests for vision, shamanic workshops, educational publications and ceremonies honoring life passages.

WAKAN Membership: After twenty-five years the Wakan Community continues to live and grow with new developments and work in the world. Membership of $35 supports us in making a monthly contribution to our extended Huichol family in Mexico helping with medical supplies for elders and school costs for younger generations. Wakan also serves as fiduciary for several small organizations that provide direct services to Native People here in the Bay Area, in

Meso-America and in Canada and South America. Wakan also offers quarterly Drum and Dessert Gatherings that are open to all interested parties.

Membership contributions allow Tom to be out in the world representing membership in providing free spiritual services to those in need through his midwifery work with dying relatives, grief work with their families, out-reach to places like the Native American group of San Quentin prisoners, and to various groups and individuals working in support of indigenous rights and environmental sustainability He makes home visits to the sick and elderly which in many instances has no financial recompense.

Without the support of Wakan membership dues and the extra monthly support of members of the Contributors Group there would not be the wind under Tom's wings that enables him to do what he does. Your membership support keeps the wind flowing. Contributions to Wakan can be sent to: Treasurer Nancy Binzen, Box 823, Woodacre, CA 94973. If you would like to join the Contributors Group, contact Nancy at nancy@wisdomtracks.com.

To receive *Wakan Talking* email updates contact leonard@leinow.com.

About the author

   Tom Pinkson, Ph.D., serves as a bridge builder, translating indigenous wisdom into a modern context bringing forth the intelligence and creativity of spiritual awakening, emotional wellbeing, and living in sustainable balance with Mother Earth and the Circle of Life.

   He is a psychologist, sacred storyteller, spiritual guide, author, musician, ceremonial retreat and vision-fast leader and a devoted grandfather. Tom helped start the first at-home Hospice in the United States. Prior to that, he started a successful wilderness treatment program for heroin addicts.

   For 32 years Tom worked with terminally ill

children at the Center for Attitudinal Healing in California, successfully integrating the wisdom teachings of the Huichol and other spiritual teachers into the world of the practicing psychologist. The founder of Wakan, a nonprofit organization committed to restoring the sacred in daily life, he lives in Northern California with his wife of 46 years Andrea Danek.

Tom helps people wake up and connect to deeper, authentic being, exploring how to live, love and work from the holy place of soul. He helps people remember we are all sacred, worthy, luminous beings; that we are love and our love is for giving.

Email: tompinkson@gmail.com
Websites: drtompinkson.com, www.nierica.com/
facebook.com/SacredLiving
and visit my on-line store.

Apology Note

In the many years of research and reading that underlies the writing of this book I excitedly took many notes scribbled down on various bits of paper. Unfortunately most of these notes were lost when it came time to cite the sources from which quotes and references were drawn. I apologize for this omission.

What I can offer is a bibliography of books and sources from which I drew, which you also can access should you desire more information or to check the details of research that I presented. Thank you for your understanding.

Especially helpful for science and health-related research:

Buddha's Brain and Hardwiring Happiness: The New Brain Science of Contentment, Calm and Confidence by Rick Hanson;

The HeartMath Solution: The Institue of HeartMath's Revolutionary Program for Engaging the Power of the Heart's Itelligence by Childre, Martin and Beech;

Authentic Happiness: Using the New Positive Psychology to Realize Your Potential for Lasting Fulfillment by Martin Seligman.

Bibliography

Albom, Mitch. *Tuesdays With Morrie.*

Arrien, Angeles. *The Second Half of Life.*

Baker, Beth, *Old Age in a New Age.*

Balsekar, Ramesh. *Consciousness Speaks.*

Bianchi, Eugene. *Aging as a Spiritual Journey.*

Bolen, Jean Shinoda (2003). *Crones Don't Whine.*

Bolen, Jean Shinoda. *Goddesses in Older Women.*

Carlson, Richard and Shield, Benjamin. *Healers on Healing*

Chinen, Allan. *In The Ever After.*

Cohen, A., *Living Enlightenment: A Call for Evolution Beyond Ego.*

Ford, Debbie. *The Dark Side of the Light Chasers: Reclaiming Your Power, Creativity, Brilliance, and Dreams.*

Gutmann, David. *Reclaimed Powers.*

Hillman, James. "Senex and Puer" in Puer Papers.

Hillman, James. *The Force of Character.*

Groff, Stanislav. *Spiritual Emergency...When Personal Transformation Becomes a Crisis.*

Jones, Terry. *Elder : A spiritual alternative to being elderly.*

Jones, Terry. *The Elder Within: Source of Mature Masculinity.*

Kornfield, Jack. *A Path With Heart...A Guide Through the Perils and Promises of Spiritual Life.*

Lakritz, Kenneth R and Knoblauch, *Elders on Love*

Leder, Drew. *Spiritual Passages.*

Levine, Stephen. *Who Dies: An Investigation of Conscious Living and Conscious Dying.*

Levinson, Daniel J. *The Seasons of a Man's Life.*

Friedan, Betty, *The Fountain of Age.*

Rowe, John and Robert Kahn, *Successful Aging.*

Ram Dass, *Still Here.*

Marion Woodman, *The Crown of Age: Rewards of Conscious Aging.*

Byock, Ira, *Dying Well: Peace and Possibilities at the End of Life.*

Leider, Richard and David Shapiro, *Something to Live For.*

Remen, Rachel, *My Grandfather's Blessings.*

Thomas, William, *What are Old People For? How Elders Will Save the World.*

Atchley, Robert, *Spirituality and Aging.*

Carter, Jimmy, *The Virtues of Aging.*

Chinen, Allan B., *In the Ever After: Fairy Tales and the Second Half of Life.*

Chittister, Joan, *The Gift of Years: Growing Older Gracefully.*

Chopra, Deepak, *Grow Younger, Live Longer.*

Cohen, Gene, *The Creative Age: Awakening Human Potential in the Second Half of Life.*

Doidge, Norman, *The Brain That Changes Itself.*

Dychtwald, Ken, and Daniel Kadlec, *A New Purpose: Redefining Money, Family, Work, Retirement and Success.*

Dychtwald, Ken, *Age Power: How the 21sCentury Will Be Ruled by the New Old.*

Freedman, Marc, *Encore: Finding Work that Matters in the Second Half of Life.*

Freedman, Marc, *Prime Time: How Baby.*

Emmons, Robert, *thanks! How the new science of gratitude can make you happier.*

Boomers Will Revolutionize Retirement and Transform America.

Emmons, Robert, *The Psychology of Ultimate Concerns.*

Goleman, Daniel, *Emotional Intelligence.*

Goleman, Daniel, *Social Intelligence.*

Hillman, James, *The Force of Character and the Lasting Life.*

Lawrence-Lightfoot, Sara, *The Third Chapter: Passion, Risk, and Adventure in the 25 Years After 50.*

Kelley, Tim, *True Purpose.*

Leder, Drew, *Spiritual Passages.*

Marohn, Stephanie, *Audacious Aging.*

Milstein, Mike, *Resilient Aging: Making the Most of Your Older Years.*

Moody, Harry, *The Five Stages of the Soul.*

Roszak, Theodore, *America the Wise.*

Stone, Marika and Howard, *Too Young To Retire: 101 Ways to Start the Rest of Your Life.*

Tafford, Abigail, *My Time: Making the Most of the Rest of Your Life.*

Vaillant, George, *Aging Well: Surprising Guideposts to a Happier Life.*

Weil, Andrew, *Healthy Aging: A Lifelong Guild to Your Physical and Spiritual Well-Being.*

Palmer, Parker J: *A Hidden Wholeness: The Journey Toward An Undivided Life.*

Robinson, John. *Death of a Hero. Birth of the Soul. Answering the Call of Midlife.*

Sadler, William, *The Third Age.*

Schachter-Shalomi, Zalman. *Ageing to Sageing.*

Sheehy, Gail. *Understanding Men's Passages: Discovering the New Map of Men's Lives.*

Simmons, Leo. *The Role of the Aged in Primitive Society.*

Suzuki, David and Peter Knudtson. *Wisdom of the Elders.*

Thomas, William H: *What Are Old People For?: How Elders Will Save the World.*

Tzu, Ram *No Way for the Spiritually "Advanced."*

Woodman, Marion. *The Crown of Age.*

Ram Dass, *Conscious Aging.*

Dr. Toni LaMotta, *Spirituality of Aging.*